Communications
in Computer and Information Science   183

Maristella Matera   Gustavo Rossi (Eds.)

Trends in Mobile Web Information Systems

MobiWIS 2013 International Workshops
Paphos, Cyprus, August 26-28, 2013
Revised Selected Papers

Springer

Volume Editors

Maristella Matera
Politecnico di Milano
Dipartimento di Elettronica, Informazione e Bioingegneria
P.zza Leonardo da Vinci, 32, 20133 Milano, Italy
E-mail: maristella.matera@polimi.it

Gustavo Rossi
Universidad Nacional de La Plata
LIFIA, Facultad de Informática
50 y 115 st., first floor (1900), La Plata, Buenos Aires, Argentina
E-mail: gustavo@lifia.info.unlp.edu.ar

ISSN 1865-0929   e-ISSN 1865-0937
ISBN 978-3-319-03736-3   e-ISBN 978-3-319-03737-0
DOI 10.1007/978-3-319-03737-0
Springer Cham Heidelberg New York Dordrecht London

Library of Congress Control Number: 2013953943

CR Subject Classification (1998): H.4, D.2, C.5.3, C.2, H.3, H.5, J.1

Typesetting: Camera-ready by author, data conversion by Scientific Publishing Services, Chennai, India

Printed on acid-free paper

Springer is part of Springer Science+Business Media (www.springer.com)

Preface

Recent advances in the Web and mobile technologies provide users with new and exciting ways to execute applications in varying pervasive and ubiquitous contexts. Design and development practices, however, pose new challenges, as users demand fast, easy, and reliable access to the high volume of Web information and services from anywhere, on any device and any delivery platform. These issues are the focus of the International Conference on Mobile Web Information Systems (MobiWIS), which this year reached its tenth edition. MobiWIS aims at promoting the discussion on the state of the art in scientific and industrial research on the technologies, models, and methodologies to support information and service provisioning by means of information systems on the mobile Web.

The MobiWIS research community gathers contributions from the more traditional and well-established research fields. However, due to the increasing diffusion of mobile technologies, it is also rapidly becoming a substantial field of action for promoting innovative, advanced research lines leading to the information systems of the future. To strengthen this potential and focus on the most innovative and emerging research trends, the MobiWIS conference hosted a workshop program. Two workshops, held on August 26, provided a forum for the discussion of fresh, yet promising ideas:

- *The First International Workshop on the Future Internet of Things and Cloud (FICloud 2013)*, focusing on the Internet of Things and its relation with cloud computing
- *The 4th International Workshop on Service Discovery and Composition in Ubiquitous and Pervasive Environments (SUPE 2013)* addressing the issues that characterize automatic service composition in ubiquitous and pervasive computing

The two workshops received submissions from different countries all over the world. A rigorous review process led to the selection of 14 papers in total. This volume collects a revised version of such papers. To mirror the feedback received during the workshops, authors were asked to revise their contributions and submit the final version of their papers after the workshops took place. We believe this volume offers a picture of some of the ideas currently fermenting in the research community working on MobiWISs.

We would like to thank the people who made the publication of this volume possible. Our special thanks go to the researchers and practitioners who wrote the papers collected in this book. We are also immensely grateful to our colleagues who dedicated time and skills to organize the workshops. We thank them for their valuable effort in attracting contributions, selecting high-quality research papers, and reliably setting up and managing the workshop programs. Their work strongly contributed to the success of the workshops program.

Finally, we sincerely thank the general chairs of MobiWIS 2013, George A. Papadopoulos, Muhammad Younas, and Elhadi Shakshuki, and the program chairs, Florian Daniel and Philippe Thiran, for their constant support and guidance.

September 2013   Maristella Matera
                                                              Gustavo Rossi

First International Workshop on the Future Internet of Things and Cloud (FiCloud 2013)

It is our pleasure to welcome you to the First International Workshop on the Future Internet of Things and Cloud (FiCloud 2013), held in conjunction with the 10th International Conference on Mobile Web Information Systems (MobiWIS 2013), during August 26–28, at the Coral Beach Hotel&Resort, Cyprus.

Advances in wireless communication and mobile networks technologies have led to many challenging problems related to global network infrastructure characterized by intelligent and self-configuring capabilities. These challenges require the design of new models, protocols, performance evaluation tools and methods and software services to keep up with their rapid evolution and increasing complexity.

The purpose of this workshop is to promote the state of the art in scientific and practical research of the IoT and cloud computing. It provides a forum for bringing together researchers and practitioners from academia, industry, and the public sector in an effort to present their research work and share research and development ideas in the area of IoT and cloud computing.

This international workshop attracted research papers both from academia and industry and from various countries around the world. These were rigorously reviewed by the scientific Program Committee members and invited reviewers. We take this opportunity to thank them for their professionalism and valuable comments made to the authors. As a result, ten papers were selected for presentation at this workshop.

Many people kindly helped us to prepare and organize the FiCloud 2013 workshop. First of all, we would like to thank the MobiWIS 2013 Workshop Coordinators, Maristella Matera and Gustavo Rossi, for their guidance and help in making the workshop a successful event. We also thank the MobiWIS 2013 PC chairs, Florian Daniel and Philippe Thiran, and the General Chair George A. Papadopoulos for their help and support. Also, we would like to give our special thanks to all who helped and contributed to the success of this workshop. Finally, we would also like to thank all the authors for selecting the FiCloud workshop to submit their contribution.

September 2013   Muhammad Younas
                                                                Irfan Awan

Organization

FiCloud 2013 Workshop Organizers

Muhammad Younas   Oxford Brookes University, UK
Irfan Awan   University of Bradford, UK

Publicity Chair

Ibrahim Ammar   University of Bradford, UK

Program Committee

Alessio Botta	Università di Napoli Federico II, Italy
Antonio Pescape	Università di Napoli Federico II, Italy
Carlos A. Iglesias	Universidad Politecnica de Madrid, Spain
Didier El Baz	LAAS-CNRS, France
Helen Karatza	Aristotle University of Thessaloniki, Greece
Makoto Ikeda	Fukuoka Institute of Technology, Japan
Payam M. Barnaghi	University of Surrey, UK
Zaki Malik	Wayne State University, Michigan, USA
Georgia Kapitsaki	University of Cyprus, Cyprus
Wei Wang	University of Surrey, UK
Karim Djemame	University of Leeds, UK
Salima Benernou	Université Paris Descartes, France
Philippe Thiran	University of Namur and Sirris, Brussels, Belgium
Daniel Neagu	University of Bradford, UK
Hong-Linh Truong	Vienna University of Technology, Austria
Zhefu Shi	Microsoft Corporation, USA
Qiang Duan	The Pennsylvania State University, USA
Khaled Salah	Khalifa University of Science, Technology and Research, UAE
Jules F. Pagna Disso	EDAS, UK

4th International Workshop on Service Discovery and Composition in Ubiquitous and Pervasive Environments (SUPE 2013)

ubiquitous and pervasive computing (UPC) is to provide computing and communication services anytime and everywhere. In ubiquitous computing (UC), the objective is to provide any mobile device with access to available services in an existing network all the time and everywhere. Pervasive computing (PC), often considered the same as ubiquitous computing in the literature, is a related concept that can be distinguished from ubiquitous computing in terms of environment conditions. The main objective in PC is to provide spontaneous services created on the fly by mobiles that interact by ad hoc connections. Interaction paradigms have been classified recently into three categories as follows: the traditional client to server paradigm (CSP) and two alternative paradigms, the adaptive services to client paradigm (SCP) and the spontaneous service emergence paradigm (SEP). SCP is more adequate to ubiquitous computing while SEP is more adequate to pervasive computing. The aim of the UPC paradigms is to move forward computational services from a conventional mode based on users/computer interactions into a new mode based on users/environment interactions. The goal of the interaction modes is to make computational services so ubiquitous/pervasive throughout a distributed environment that they become transparent to the human user.

Building ubiquitous and pervasive applications to carry out these modes of interaction requires new methodologies and architectures that involve many distributed and dynamically interacting components. To meet these requirements, service composition plays a fundamental role and automation is essential to improve the speed and efficiency of users' requests. Service composition is the act of taking several distributed computational components or services and handling them together to meet the needs of a given user. It should be noted that automatic or dynamic service composition must involve the automatic selection, composition, and cooperation of appropriate services to perform and satisfy the user task, given a high-level description of the task's objective.

The current approaches and methodologies for addressing these above issues can be classified into two major research directions. The first direction addresses semantic languages to specify and describe application components, including complex planning mechanisms that utilize these descriptions to generate the whole application or composite service. In other words, this research direction is trying to define languages to formally specify services, invocation mechanisms, and composite services. The second direction aims to develop architectures that enable scalable, fault tolerance, and adaptive applications in dynamic environments.

The SUPE 2013 workshop co-located with MobiWIS 2013 was intended to serve as a forum and bring together researchers and engineers in both academia and industry to exchange ideas, share experiences, and report original works on all aspects of service discovery and composition in ubiquitous and pervasive environments.

Articles presented at the SUPE 2013 workshop provided a comprehensive overview of the key topics and perspectives regarding UPC issues. Four articles were selected, several considering systems modeling and service-oriented concepts in UPC environments.

In the first article, A. Almutairi and F. Siewe present a control model of a U-learning system using CA-UCON. It is used to model a U-learning system and analyze its properties through simulations. In other words, the authors illustrate, via certain scenarios, how U-learning system properties can be validated using the execution environment of CCA.

M. Madkour et al. in the second article introduce an approach for context-aware service selection using QoS and user preferences. In this approach, QoS parameters and policies are used in both service selection and adaptation processes. Preliminary results show the usefulness and the importance of QoS and user preferences in the service selection process.

in the third paper, W. Labda et al. propose a privacy-aware business processes modeling notation (PrvBPMN) in a distributed mobile context. The main aim of this work is to develop a privacy-aware service-based framework and system that could be used to model and manage emergency situations in airports.

A. Nait-Sidi-Moh et al. in the fourth article introduce a service-oriented platform integrating geofencing techniques for real-time tracking of mobile devices. The authors focus mainly on the development and integration of a geofencing application and its related services into a unified platform in order to allow virtual perimeters to be defined and mobile devices to be tracked. Some results are presented to show the impact of using geofencing concepts on safety and road transport efficiency.

The papers presented at the SUPE workshop cover several approaches and relevant activities in the design of middleware, protocols and algorithms, and service-oriented architectures for UPC environments. We hope that the readers can benefit from the perspectives developed in these papers and will contribute to this exciting area of research.

The SUPE 2013 co-chairs would like to thank all the authors who submitted their papers to the workshop. We are also very obliged to the referees for their comments and feedbacks to authors. We would principally like to express our gratitude to the workshops chairs and organizers of MobiWIS 2013 for their assistance during the preparation, and for giving the authors the opportunity to present their work in Springer's proceedings for the MobiWIS 2013 Workshops.

September 2013   Mohamed Bakhouya
Jaafar Gaber
Maxime Wack

Organization

SUPE 2013 Workshop Organizers

Mohamed Bakhouya	Aalto University, School of Engineering, Finland
Jaafar Gaber	Université de Technologie de Belfort-Montbeliard, France
Maxime Wack	Université de Technologie de Belfort-Montbeliard, France

Program Committee

Juliette Marais	Laboratoire LEOST, INRETS Villeneuve D'Ascq, France
Ridha Bouallegue	ESTI, Tunis
Mika Luimula	CENTRIA, Finland
Ahmed Nait Sidi Moh	Université de Picardie Jules Verne, France
Katarzyna Wac	University of Geneva, Switzerland
Chung-Wei Hang	North Carolina State University, USA
Jalal Al-Muhtadi	King Saud University, Saudi Arabia
Vincenzo De Florio	University of Antwerp, Belgium
Pradeep Murukannaiah	North Carolina State University, USA
Mohamed Nemiche	Ibn Zohr University, Morocco
Walid Chainbi	University of Sousse, Tunisia
Pi-Chung Wang	National Chung Hsing University, Taiwan
Antonio Coronato	Institute for High-Performance Computing and Networking, Italy
Tuan Nguyen	University of Information Technology, Vietnam

QoS of Context-Aware Transactions in Pervasive Computing and IoT

Muhammad Younas[1] and Irfan Awan[2]

[1]Department of Computing and Communication Technologies
Oxford Brookes University, Oxford, UK
m.younas@brookes.ac.uk
[2]Department of Computing,
University of Bradford, Bradford, UK
i.u.awan@bradford.ac.uk

Abstract of the Invited Talk: Technological developments in mobile devices, software systems, and network communication have led to the development of a pervasive computing infrastructure which creates an environment where computing is available everywhere. The goal is to provide useful information and services that adapt to the given context such as user's situation, time, location, and network conditions. Various developments have been made in the design and development of pervasive computing technologies and their applications. Recently, the Internet of Things (IoT) has emerged as a dynamic network of physical "things" which are seamlessly integrated into the Internet. With the support of IoT, pervasive computing can be further enhanced through the integration of and communication among things which have network identities, physical attributes, intelligent interfaces as well as computing capabilities [1]. The synergy of IoT, Web of Things [4], and pervasive computing has interesting real life applications, for example, checking the hydration level of plants and watering them when necessary or helping the emergency services such as road side accident and traffic management.

Pervasive computing and IoT face various research challenges such as performance, reliability, security, privacy, data management, and usability among others. In this talk, we will discuss the issue of context-aware transactions and their Quality of Service (QoS) [5] which are central to the study of performance, reliability and consistency of pervasive and IoT applications. The talk is based on our work published in [2, 3] in which we have designed and developed new models and protocols for context-aware transactions and QoS of their mobility management. Basically, the objective of employing transactions is to provide pervasive and IoT applications with consistent and reliable execution despite failures of mobile devices, computer systems, and network communication. Our work enhances transactions with context-awareness such that they can dynamically adapt to user's needs and network conditions. In this talk we also touch on identifying future research issues which are specific to context-aware transactions in IoT environment. These include, for instance, handling of physical devices in addition to data and software applications; dealing with cancellation or compensation of transactions in IoT; fault tolerance and recovery management.

Keywords: Transactions, Context-awareness, Pervasive Computing,
Internet of Things, Quality of service, Modelling.

References

1. Vermesan, O., et al. 2009. Internet of Things Strategic Research Roadmap. *European Research Cluster on the Internet of Things, Cluster Strategic Research Agenda*
2. Younas, M., Mostefaoui, S. K. 2011. A New Model for Context-aware Transactions in Mobile Services. Personal and Ubiquitous Computing, Vol. 15(8), 821-831
3. Younas, M., Awan, I. 2013. Mobility Management Scheme for Context-aware Transactions in Pervasive and Mobile Cyberspace. IEEE Transactions on Industrial Electronics, Vol. 60(3), 1108-1115
4. Grønli, T-M., Ghinea, G., Younas, M. 2013. A Lightweight Architecture for the Web-of-Things. In Proceeding of the 10th International Conference Mobile Web Information Systems (MobiWIS 2013), Paphos, Cyprus, August 26-29, 2013. Springer LNCS, ISBN 978-3-642-40275-3, 248-259
5. Zheng, J., Simplot-Ryl, D., Bisdikian, C., Mouftah, H.T. 2011. Guest Editorial - The Internet of Things, IEEE Communications Magazine, November, 30-31

Table of Contents

First International Workshop on the Future Internet of Things and Cloud (FiCloud 2013)

Fourth International Workshop on Service Discovery and Composition in Ubiquitous and Pervasive Environments (SUPE 2013)

How the Internet of Things Will Change the User Experience Status Quo

Noel Portugal

Oracle Corporation, Applications User Experience, Austin, Texas, USA
noel.portugal@oracle.com

Abstract. The Internet of Things (IoT) will find its way into the way we work. As sensors and other connected devices invade our homes and places of work, we will expect an increase in new emergent ways to harness all this data to our advantage. Having intelligent context engines will be the glue that brings disparate data streams together. As we learn how we can use this data it will change the way we work and interact with our systems, effectively changing the User Experience (UX) status quo. This paper will explore the opportunities that IoT brings by collecting user data to help determine its context and offer a more compelling User Experience.

Keywords: IoT, UX, Location, Sensors, Context engines, Big data.

1   Introduction

We can define User Experience as the complete experience to accomplish a task. A successful User Experience will enable users to produce creative insights, make timely decisions, and complete their work in an accurate and efficient manner.

In the current state of the User Experience we tend to rely on the contextual information provided by the system. This information is limited by explicit data previously recorded into the system. Data such as profile, role, and access control lists (ACL) help the user access relevant information stored in the system. This information may not be enough to help the user accomplish all necessary tasks effectively.

We currently rely on manually captured data to make informed decisions in our day to day work. We also have had the need for personal or executive assistants to help us accomplish time consuming work. Work such as meeting scheduling, calendaring, meeting notes and material distribution. As the knowledge worker task-force increases and organization budget restrictions increase it might not be possible to have this kind of aid for all users.

In the past it has been widely discussed how smart connected devices can help the manufacturing industries and any industry in general using Enterprise Resource Planning (ERP) based systems. Tasks such as real-time inventory tracking, temperature monitors, and resource allocation have been previously discussed as prime candidates of the Internet of Things applications.

M. Matera and G. Rossi (Eds.): MobiWIS 2013 Workshops, CCIS 183, pp. 1–5, 2013.

A sensor or detector measures physical quantities and converts them into a signal that can typically be read by an electronic instrument. Internet connected sensors and devices are what has become known as the Internet of Things. The next frontier is the application of these connected devices in our day to day work. The Internet of Things expands a brand new way to enhance the applications User Experience. Sensors and other connected devices can collect invaluable information that can collectively help us work in a more efficient way. Location data will be one of the most important measures to deliver the right content at the right time and to the right person.

Physical presence is one of the most important metrics used to provide a better User Experience using the Internet of Things. Indoor activities and interactions with other users will prove to be of great insight when analyzed by smart systems. By tracking the user inside movements and interactions with other users, intelligent systems will be able to make better recommendations on how to accomplish tasks in a more efficient way.

Raw data coming directly from these interconnected devices will not be completely valuable unless it is first uploaded to a global repository and processed by a context engine. A context engine is needed to help make sense of all this information and should make smart decisions based on predefined rules. As context engines mature they will also learn patterns and make appropriate suggestions based on historical data and complex algorithms.

2   The Cloud and Big Data

As more devices are enabled with connected capabilities the need for capable repositories that can be easily accessed by any system and with the right access authorization is crucial. This global repository solution is the Cloud, which is a network of computer systems. The Cloud has become the de-facto home of Internet of Things repositories.

Current advances in location technology are making it easier to track an individual's physical presence. The key to these advances is not just better Global Positioning Systems (GPS), but a combination of data coming from different sensors and devices such as Wifi routers and smartphone sensors such as gyroscopes, compasses, and barometers (to detect altitude). The data provided by these sensors can yield a more precise location even if the user is indoors. Radio frequency technologies such as passive or active Radio-Frequency Identification (RFID) and Bluetooth sensors could also help provide accuracy. Near Field Communications (NFC) is another alternative to keep track of physical presence. In the case of NFC the user has to implicitly log its location [1].

As more Internet of Things devices are added to our ecosystem it is important to maintain a standard way of communicating with each other. A possible way to do so would be to follow Representational State Transfer (REST) style architectures applied to each device. Each device can potentially call any other device by using any of the REST-style methods such as GET, POST, PUT, and DELETE. Any connected device could potentially be accessed inside the local network (Intranet) as well as from the Internet, with the assumption that security protocols have been set in place.

As sensors upload data at exponentially faster rates the remote Cloud repository becomes a Big Data source. Big Data is defined as a large collection of data sets that conventionally are not easily processed by traditional relational database tools. The data collected by Big Data repositories on the Cloud do not always necessarily have to adhere to ACID (Atomicity, Consistency, Isolation, Durability) database properties. Instead data stored in Big Data datasets can yield better results when properly analyzed for trends and patterns.

3   Context Engine

An intelligent system is needed in order to effectively use the massive amount of data generated by sensors and other IoT devices. These devices are constantly uploading data to Big Data repositories. This system is what I call a Context Engine. A Context Engine has the job to provide relevant information to a user according to that user context. This context is created by a combination of data provided by the following:

- Explicit data from the system (profile, access control).
- Implicit data collected from the user local environment (cookies, local time).
- User based rules and workflows.
- Data collected by various sensors and devices (location, heat).

The Context Engine is responsible for providing meaningful connections and suggestions. As more data is added into the system, the engine will have better recommendations. The context engine also has the capability to reach into other

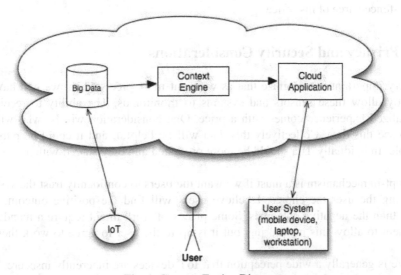

Fig. 1. Context Engine Diagram

systems to collect data to compliment its output suggestions. The architecture of the Context Engine is generally an independent system that can be queried by other systems. Communication is done by common internet protocols using a REST API architecture with proper authentication methods.

4   Use Case

The following example provides a scenario for the ability of IoT to track physical presence in the workplace: A user comes to the office in the morning. As he enters his office the lights come on and temperature is automatically adjusted to the user's predefined preference. Since the system knows who he is and his role it will present the user with the day's tasks to accomplish. As the day goes by a co-worker stops by his desk and ask a few questions. Since the system knows who the co-worker is it will display outstanding activities that involve that co-worker. Now the user has a reminder to inquire about these activities and set up a chance to follow up.

After lunch the user attends a meeting in a conference room. The conference room has sensors that can tell who is in the meeting. All meeting attendees are automatically added to a virtual conference where they can review the material in their own systems and make annotations that will be shared with the team in real time. The system can send meeting notes, recordings, and materials discussed to the people who could not attend the meeting.

Before the day is over, another user happens to walk by the user's desk. These two users do not know each other. The system recognizes the individual and prompts the user to inquire about a project which both have common interests but never had to physically meet and discuss. Anytime the user walks away from his office, his system and access to records are automatically locked. These are only available while he is in the geo-fenced area of his office.

5   Privacy and Security Considerations

It is very important to recognize that as we want more precise data, we will have to explicitly allow these sensors and systems to monitor us. The ability to receive a personalized experience comes with a price. One consideration will be who will be able to see this data. Collectively this data will be helpful, and it could be publicly available. Individually data should be more protected and only shared with authorized parties.

An opt-in mechanism is a must if we want the users to confidently trust the system. By giving the user the choice, I believe users will find the positive outcomes far greater than the negative outcomes. Some places of work might require a mandatory agreement to allow this monitoring, but it is up to the user to agree to work there or not.

There is generally a wide perception that IoT devices are inherently insecure. This notion comes from the fact that these new internet citizens lack the human factor to establish communications and can be completely autonomous. As a starting point to resolve this the IoT need to adhere to existing security mechanism used on the web. Authentication methods such as OpenId, as well as authorization methods like oAuth should be used whenever required. Transport Layer Security (TLS) and its predecessor, Secure Sockets Layer (SSL) protocols should also be used to provide secured communications on the internet.

Legal frameworks have been suggested to assure that IoT devices will comply with paradigms of IT governance, ensuring resilience to attacks, data authentication, access control and client privacy [2].

6   Conclusion

The Internet of Things is poised to change the way we currently work. It will not be just one single device or sensor that will give the necessary information. It will be a collection of explicit and implicit data collected by smart devices that will be able to provide better personal context to our systems. The current state of User Experience is limited by the system explicit constraints. As we feed the system with more relevant data, the user experiences will be more rewarding.

References

1. Teixeira, T., Dublon, G., Savvides, A.: A Survey of Human-Sensing: Methods for Detecting Presence, Count, Location, Track, and Identity. ACM Computing Surveys V(N) (20YY)
2. Weber, R.H.: Internet of Things – New security and privacy challenges

Scalable Extensible Secured and Safe Smart Gateway Platform Solution for Smart Grid/ Energy and IoT

Vishwapathi Rao Tadinada[1] and Kwok Wu[2]

[1] Freescale Semiconductors, India
tv.rao@freescale.com
[2] Freescale Semiconductors, USA
kwok.wu@freescale.com

Abstract. IoT is here to stay, while the use of IPv6 is imperative to connect all devices globally via Internet, where security and networking safety is of primary concern.

This paper takes the example of the multi-billion dollar Smart Grid market and describes the security concerns for the applications in this market: Smart Meter, Data Concentrator, Sub Station Automation and the cloud-connected SCADA, Supervisory Control and Data Acquisitions network. For each of the segments/application the security concerns are analyzed and solutions to these concerns are proposed whilst addressing the IoT market opportunities. The four pillars of network security viz. Integrity, Availability, Confidentiality, Non-repudiation as specified by NIST SP 800 82 [1] , NERC and IEEE are addressed in the proposed solutions. Apart from security; performance and scalability are given due importance and consideration both from software and hardware perspective in the proposed platform solution.

Freescale's M2M (Machine-to-Machine) and IoT end-to-end security solutions provided in this paper can be extended to other areas like smart energy, smart health, smart transportation, smart factory, enterprise and residential (smart home) and make connected intelligence a reality.

1 Introduction

This paper takes a closer look at the security concerns at the communication layer of the Smart Grid which is expected to be predominantly IP based network as shown in Figure 1. As the data is transmitted over Internet it has to be assured security in terms of Data Integrity, Confidentiality and Non Repudiation. All devices must be protected against denial of service attacks, cyber attacks, vulnerabilities and exploits. They should also be protected from malformed and bad traffic. Every IP address is susceptible to attacks and must be protected.

Smart Meters, Concentrators, Transmission line sensors are deployed out in the open and thus must be protected from physical attacks and tampering. Such attempts have to be detected with help of sensors and reported to the Utility. Trusted boot and secure architecture must be provided to protect against unauthorized or malicious firmware upgrade.

M. Matera and G. Rossi (Eds.): MobiWIS 2013 Workshops, CCIS 183, pp. 6–16, 2013.

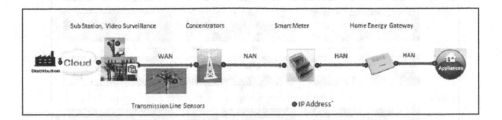

Fig. 1. End-to-End Security in the Smart Grid

Reliable two way communication is essential for effective functioning of the Smart Grid. Reliability and redundancy can be provided by having a mesh topology at the Concentrator. Additional reliability of communication can be achieved by having two WAN connections at the Concentrator and Sub Stations for load balancing and fail over. Reliability can be further enhanced by implementing RAID 5, Redundant Array of Independent Disks (https://en.wikipedia.org/wiki/RAID) on upstream device to protect loss of transient data.

This paper analyzes the security concerns across the Smart Grid hierarchy shown in Figure 2 and proposes platform solutions in form of Freescale hardware and software. Some examples of platform solutions covering various aspects of security discussed in this paper are:

1. Smart Meter: Low footprint IP Stack with 6LoWPAN, Firewall and IPSec-IKEv2 running on Freescale MC1322x.
2. Concentrator: IP Stack on Concentrator with 802.15.4 and 802.3 running on Freescale P1025 QorIQ.
3. Home Energy Gateway on Freescale MPC8308 with WiFi and Security Software.
4. Utility and Sub Station Servers with Security, Load balancer, virtualization software running on Freescale P4080 QorIQ.

2 Securing Communication on the Smart Grid

This section covers the various layers of Smart Grid Hierarchical Architecture, security concerns for each layer and platform solutions for each. Smart Grid security can be divided in the following segments/application blocks as shown in Figure 2:

1. Neighborhood Area Network- NAN (Smart Meter to Concentrator)
2. Home Area Network- HAN (Appliances to Smart Meter or Home Energy Gateway)
3. Wide Area Network- WAN (Concentrator to Sub Station/Utility)

Each of these layers is described in the upcoming sub-sections in terms of their typical deployment, network topology, communication technology, security

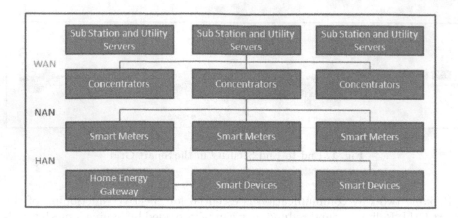

Fig. 2. Smart Grid Hierarchical Architecture

concerns for the devices in each segment and protecting the data that is being communicated. A platform solution detailing Freescale hardware and software addressing security issues is proposed.

2.1 Securing NAN (Metrology-to-Concentrator)

NAN, Neighborhood Area network that connects the Smart Meter to the Concentrator is perhaps the most challenging in terms of vulnerability and security solutions because of the following reasons:

1. Varied communication technologies options available: WiMAX, 3/4G, 802.15.4, PLC. Though multiple technologies are available, most of them are wireless and suffer the drawbacks of the wireless communication where the data can be sniffed and tampered with.
2. Low memory and other hardware resource constraints on the Smart Meter limit the feasibility of a robust security solution and restrict the options available for connection technologies.
3. Both Smart Meter and Concentrators are deployed outdoors and are susceptible to physical attacks

These factors make NAN the weakest link the Smart Grid and thus all factors impacting security need to be taken into considerations and addressed carefully.

This section takes 802.15.4 as example of communication between Smart Meter and Concentrators and discusses the security issues and demonstrates how they can be addressed. The same can be applied to other modes of communication.

2.1.1 Platform Solution for Smart Meter
Since adoption of IPv6 is inevitable, in this example 6LoWPAN/802.15.4 running on Freescale MC1322x is proposed as a platform solution. The IP stack can

be enhanced with rich security features integrating Freescale's VortiQa[2] Firewall, IPSec[3] and IKEv2 [4] as shown in Figure 3. However, since the flash and RAM on the board are less, light-weight version the security application to fit into sub 100 K ROM and sub 100 K RAM is used. Further, VaultIC from InsideeSecure (http://www.insidesecure.com/eng/Products/Secure-Solutions/Secure-solutions-products) can be used to secure the keys and certificates on the Smart Meter.

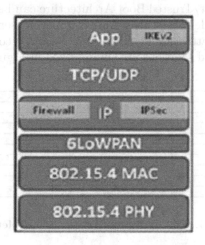

Fig. 3. IP Stack on Smart Meter with 6LoWPAN, Firewall and IPSec-IKEv2 running on Freescale MC1322x

2.1.2 Network Topology and IP Addressing: NAN
For NAN, the Concentrator is considered to be the focal point, 802.15.4 coordinator, a Full Functional Device (FFD) and the Smart Meter a Reduced Functional Device (RFD) with routing function. All Smart Meters in a given area or building are fully meshed with Concentrator as Coordinator. The Concentrator assigns DHCP v6 IP addresses to the *Smart* Meters.

2.1.3 Security on Smart Meter
Smart Meter comes preloaded with shared keys or certificates. Alternatively keys or certificates can be distributed in an out-of-band trusted mechanism. Since IP address at the Smart Meter is dynamically assigned Internet Remote Access Client IRAC, can be used for IKE exchanges. IKEv2 is used for Identity protection and for establishing Encryption and Authentication keys for the IPSec tunnel between the Smart Meter and Concentrator. This combination IKE and IPSec provides a secured NAN channel with data confidentiality and integrity. Sequence number in the IKE and IPSec help protect against replay and man in the middle attacks. Digital Signatures can be used for non-repudiation. Access policies or Access Control List can be configured on the Firewall to allow

only traffic from HAN to the Utility and vice-a-versa to pass through Smart Meter. Self traffic can be limited only to allow IKE, DNS, DHCP traffic from Concentrator to self and vice-a-versa. Since the Smart Meter is expected to be actively communicating with the HAN devices, ACL should allow traffic from HAN to Self and vice-a-versa. DoS/Cyber-Attack check can be enabled on the Firewall to protect the Smart Meter from well known attacks like Ping Flood, Syn Flood, LAND Attacks; Smurf Attacks. Any such attack detected should then be reported to Utility.

Freescale Secure Boot/Trusted Boot Architecture can be used to prevent malicious firmware upgrade. Freescale's Anti Tampering sensors can be used to protect from physical attacks and tampering. Security concerns at the Smart Meter and the suggested solutions are summarized in Figure 4

Security Consideration	Proposed Solution
Data Integrity/Authentication	VortiQa IPSec/IKEv2
Data Confidentiality/Encryption	VortiQa IPSec/IKEv2
Non-Repudiation	VortiQa IPSec/IKEv2
Reply-Man-in-the-Middle Attacks	VortiQa IPSec/IKEv2
Identity Check	VortiQa IPSec/IKEv2
Availability/Denial of Service	VortiQa Firewall
Access Control	VortiQa Firewall
Malicious firmware upgrade	Freescale's Secure Boot Arch
Tampering Physical attacks	Freescale's Anti Tampering Sensors

Fig. 4. Security Solution on the Smart Meter

2.2   Securing Home Area Network (HAN)

Home Area Network (HAN)has multiple smart automated appliances like HVAC (Heating, Ventilation and Air Conditioning), washing/dryer machines, smart plugs, lighting and multimedia connected to Smart Meter and/or Home Energy Gateway, then the Smart Meters from multiple households are connected to the data concentrator in the Neighborhood Area Network (NAN) for Advanced Metering Infrastructure (AMI). These appliances can be monitored and managed to use energy efficiently. This connected intelligence is provided by Freescale's Smart Energy Solutions.

As shown in Figure 5, all smart appliances are connected to the Home Energy Gateway communicating over wireless 802.15.4. The Home Energy Gateway in turn connects to Internet via 3G/LTE or DSL. Optionally it can act as an 802.11.x Wireless AP.

2.2.1   Platform Solution for Home Energy Gateway
Freescale offers a converged architecture networked Smart Energy Gateway on MPC8308 [5], offering seamless connectivity with TCP/IP, 802.11n and Zig-Bee. VortiQa Software offers Firewall, NAT, Intrusion Detection and Prevention (IDS/IPS), Application Identification/Monitoring System (AIS) and IPSec and IKE security services. Details of this solution are available at (http://www.youtube.com/watch?v=ZlwivEjW2tk)

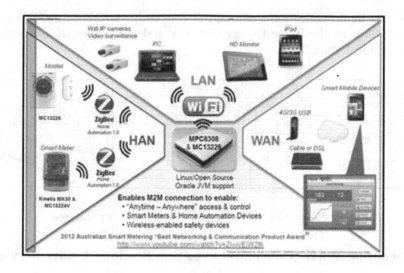

Fig. 5. Home Energy Gateway on Freescale MPC 8308

2.2.2 Network Topology and IP Addressing

As shown in Figure 6, all smart appliances are connected to the Home Energy Gateway communicating over wireless 802.15.4. Smart metering connectivity is achieved via ZigBee SE 1 or MBus. Smart appliances are managed via ZigBee HA1.0.

On the WAN side the Home Energy Gateway connects to Internet via 3G/LTE or DSL using DHCP whereby, IP Address is dynamically assigned by the service provider.

Freescale wireless gateway can optionally act as an 802.11.x Wireless AP on the LAN side. The AP provide IP addresses to the LAN devices like laptops, tablets.

Freescale wireless Gateway also runs on P1010, i.Mx platforms with Trusted Architecture and Trusted Boot.

2.2.3 Security on Smart Energy Gateway

The remote monitoring, control and management of all in-home Smart Appliances happens through the Smart Energy Gateway. This data is sensitive and private and thus has to be provided security while traversing the Internet. This is achieved by establishing an encrypted secure channel for this traffic over the WAN. VortiQa IPSec/IKEv2 or SSL can be used to provide this. In addition to confidentiality this solution provides integrity, identity protection, non-repudiation and protection against replay and man in the middle attacks. Tight access control policies can be implemented using VortiQa Firewall to allow only authorized traffic to and through the gateway. DoS/Cyber Attack check can be enabled on the Firewall to protect the Home Energy Gateway and the internal network from well know D/DOS attacks. VortiQa AIS can be used to control/rate-limit application traffic eg P2P, Social Networking Application. Security concerns at the Home Energy Gateway and the suggested solutions are summarized in Figure 6.

Security Consideration	Proposed Solution
Data Integrity/Authentication	VortiQa IPSec/IKEv2
Data Confidentiality/Encryption	VortiQa IPSec/IKEv2
Non-Repudiation	VortiQa IPSec/IKEv2
Reply-Man-in-the-Middle Attacks	VortiQa IPSec/IKEv2
Identity Check	VortiQa IPSec/IKEv2
Availability/Denial of Service	VortiQa Firewall
Access Control	VortiQa Firewall
NAT	VortiQa Firewall
Application Detection and Control	VortiQa AIS
Trusted/Secure Boot	Freescale's Secure Boot Arch
Anti Tampering	Freescale's Anti Tampering Sensors

Fig. 6. Summary of Security on the Home Energy Gateway

2.3   Securing WAN (Concentrator-to-Sub Station/ Utility Servers)

The communication between Concentrator and the Sub Station can happen on one of the several WAN technologies like WiMAX, 3G/4G, PLC. This communication is predominantly IP based and data travels over the Internet. This sensitive bi-directional data i.e. from the Smart Meter to Utility and vice-a-versa has to be protected from eavesdroppers to maintain confidentiality and integrity. As this link is critical to transfer real time data, to ensure reliability it recommended to have a fail over connection. Critical messages from/to the meter must be prioritized over other traffic. The transient data on the concentrator has to be protected in case of crashes. Further the Concentrator has to be protected from DOS attacks, bad traffic and unauthorized access. As in case of Smart Meters, since Concentrators are deployed outdoors they have to be protected against physical attacks and tampering.

2.3.1   Platform Solution for Concentrator
Freescale P1025 QorIQ[6] processor 667MHz/800MHz dual core device with memory up to 128 MB of NOR/NAND flash memory, Security Accelerator, running VortiQa Firewall, IPSec, IKEv2 and Application Identification Software can be used as a Concentrator as shown in Figure 7 delivering security and high performance.

This platform has 3G, WiFi, Zigbee WSN communication and 3 Giga-bit Ethernet capable ports to enable WAN/LAN communications and can communicate with Smart Metering devices via the industry standard Device Language Message Specification (DLMS) (IEC 62056). It offers Zigbee wireless connectivity to meters and 3G Broadband to Utility server. This device has energy efficient passive cooled design and has ruggedized, weather resistant construction.

2.3.2   Platform Solution for Sub Station/Utility Servers
Freescale P4080[7] QorIQ processor 1.5 GHz eight core device with Security Accelerator and Packet Matching Engine, running VortiQa Firewall, IPSec, IKEv2

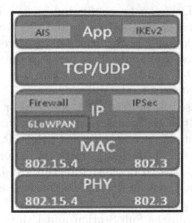

Fig. 7. IP Stack with 802.15.4 and 802.3 on Concentrator

and AIS-Application Identification Software can be used as a Utility Server. DPAA on P4080 delivers high performance with acceleration for the following functions:

1. Packet parsing, classification, and distribution
2. Queue management for scheduling, packet sequencing, and congestion management
3. Hardware buffer management for buffer allocation and de-allocation
4. Encryption (SEC 4.0)
5. RegEx Pattern Matching (PME 2.0)

   These devices can be "clusterstered" at the utility to provide load balancing and failover for reliability and performance.

2.3.3 Network Topology and IP Addressing: WAN
The Concentrator's WAN interfaces get DHCP v6 addressed from the Sub Station. This connection can be 3G/LTE WiMAX, PLC. For greater reliability two links to the Sub Station can be provisioned using VortiQa Load Balancing and Fail Over (LBFO).

2.3.4 Security on the Concentrator and Utility Servers
Concentrator plays a key role in aggregating data form the Smart Meters within its area and propagating it upstream to Sub Station or Utility over the WAN link. This data traveling over Internet has to be encrypted for confidentiality and privacy. A secure IPSec VPN-Virtual Private Network tunnel can be established between Concentrator and Sub Station/Utility using VortiQa IPSec/IKEv2. Since IP address at Concentrator is dynamically assigned IRAC can be used for IKE exchanges. This tunnel provides data confidentiality, integrity, non-repudiation and protection against replay and man in the middle attacks.

ACL-Access Control List, can be configured on the Firewall to limit traffic from Home Area Network to the Utility and vice-a-versa to pass through Concentrator. ACL should allow traffic from Smart Meter to Concentrator and vice-a-versa to allow active communication between these devices. DoS/Cyber Attack check can be enabled on the Firewall to protect the Concentrator from attacks and report such attacks to the utility.

VortiQa AIS can be used to protect the Concentrator for bad and malicious traffic, AIS has a rich set of signatures to detect bad traffic, P2P application, vulnerabilities and exploits of protocols like HTTP, FTP, SSH. On detection of bad traffic action can be set to drop such traffic and inform utility.

Freescale Secure Boot/Trusted Boot Architecture can be used to prevent malicious firmware upgrade. Freescale's Anti Tampering sensors can be used to protect from physical attacks and tampering..

Security configuration on the Sub Station and Utility server is pretty much similar to that on the Concentrator. In cases where the WAN IP address of the Sub Station is configured manually and known to the Utility server site-to-site IPSec can be configured instead of IRAC. Though most equipment including the surveillance cameras are in premise there are relatively well covered from physical attacks it is recommended to have anti-tamper sensors. Transmission line sensors are deployed on the transmission lines. Anti tamper sensors should be used on these sensors where the lines run above ground to detect and report attack.

Quality of Service (QOS) must be configured on the Concentrator, Sub Station and Utility server to prioritize critical messaging data over other traffic.

Security concerns at the Concentrator and the proposed solutions are summarized in Figure 8.

Security Consideration	Proposed Solution	
Data Integrity/Authentication	VortiQa IPSec/IKEv2	
Data Confidentiality/Encryption	VortiQa IPSec/IKEv2	
Non-Repudiation	VortiQa IPSec/IKEv2	
Reply-Man-in-the-Middle Attacks	VortiQa IPSec/IKEv2	
Identity Check	VortiQa IPSec/IKEv2	
Availability/Denial of Service	VortiQa Firewall	
Access Control and NAT	VortiQa Firewall	QorIQ P1025 Dual-core Data Concentrator
QoS	VortiQa TM	
Application Detection and Control	VortiQa AIS	
Malicious firmware upgrade	Freescale's Secure Boot Arch	
Tampering, Physical attacks	Freescale's Anti Tampering Sensors	

Fig. 8. Security Solition on Concenretaor

3   Summing It Up

The secure platform solutions proposed in this paper facilitate distribution grid automation which provides improved monitoring and visibility of a Utility company's large distributed assets. Such remote monitoring capabilities serve as a key motivation for the Utility as it results in significantly improved ROI.

For example, AMI (Advanced Metering Infrastructure) with automated smart data concentrators and transmission line monitoring sensors can improve the business operations such as DR (Demand Response) to prevent brown-out and does not require significant behavioral change by customers. Benefits to the Utility company are: reduced downtime, faster service restorations, rapid identification of faults for preventive maintenance.

Figure 9 summarizes the Freescale's Secure Platform Solutions for Smart Grid.

Freescale Secure Platform Solutions for Smart Energy			
	Home Energy Gateway	Smart Meter	Concentrators	Distribution
Security Concern	Proposed Solution			
Data Integrity/Authentication	IPSec/IKEv2	IPSec/IKEv2	IPSec/IKEv2	IPSec/IKEv2
Data Confidentiality/Encryption	IPSec/IKEv2	IPSec/IKEv2	IPSec/IKEv2	IPSec/IKEv2
Non-Repudiation	IPSec/IKEv2	IPSec/IKEv2	IPSec/IKEv2	IPSec/IKEv2
Replay Attacks/ Man in the middle Attacks	IPSec/IKEv2	IPSec/IKEv2	IPSec/IKEv2	IPSec/IKEv2
Identity Check/Data Source Authentication	IPSec/IKEv2	IPSec/IKEv2	IPSec/IKEv2	IPSec/IKEv2
Availability/Denial Of Service	Firewall	Firewall	Firewall	Firewall
Vulnerability and Exploit	Firewall+AIS	Firewall	Firewall	Firewall+AIS
Access Control	Firewall	Firewall	Firewall	Firewall
Unauthorized Firmware Upgrade	Secure Boot Arch	Secure Boot Arch	Secure Boot Arch	Secure Boot Arch
Anti Tampering	NA	Anti Tampering Sensors	Anti Tampering Sensors	NA
Hardware Platform	MPC 8308	MC1322x	P1025	P4080

Fig. 9. Secure Platform Solutions for Smart Grid

VortiQa[2] security software Firewall, IPSec, IKE runs on standard SMP Linux and is fully integrated with PowerQUICC III and QorIQ processor architectures to deliver optimum network performance under both normal and stressful network conditions. The software is optimized to leverage SoC hardware acceleration functions of the Freescale processors, such as the security (SEC) engine for VPN processing, pattern matching engine (PME) for IPS and the data-path acceleration engine for flow management to achieve high throughput and high session rate processing to meet the demanding security, performance and scalability requirements of the Smart Grid.

4   Conclusion

This paper has covered security concerns at various layers of Smart Grid and proposed end to end high performance security solutions viewing Smart Grid as a system. The four pillars of network security (specified by NIST SP 800 82, NERC and IEEE) are addressed in the proposed platform solution:

1. Integrity: Prevent unauthorized modification of information
2. Availability: Prevent DOS (Denial of Service)and Intrusion Prevention.
3. Confidentiality: Prevent unauthorized access of information
4. Non-repudiation: Prevent denial of action.

The secured M2M, IOT solution provided here is not limited Smart Grid, this model can be adapted and extended to other applications/markets like:

1. Gas and Water distribution
2. Health, Residential and Transport
3. Factory Automation
4. Securing Enterprise and Data centers

References

1. Stouffer, K.: Guide to industrial control systems (ics) security (2011)
2. Vortiqa software for networking equipment, http://www.freescale.com.hk/files/32bit/doc/brochure/VORTOVRBR.pdf
3. Kent, R.A.S.: Security architecture for the internet protocol, rfc 2401 (1998)
4. Kaufman: Internet key exchange (ikev2) protocol, rfc 4306, (2005)
5. Mpc8308 networked smart gateway reference design, http://www.freescale.com.hk/webapp/sps/site/prod_summary.jsp?code=RDMPC8308NSG
6. Qoriq p1025 data concentrator reference design for energy management, http://www.freescale.com/webapp/sps/site/prod_summary.jsp?code=RDP1025DC&nodeId=0225E76A10&tab=Design_Support_Tab&site_preference=normal
7. P4080: Qoriq p4080/p4040/p4081 communications processors with data path, http://www.freescale.com.hk/webapp/sps/site/prod_summary.jsp?code=P4080

Empirical Evaluation and Analysis of Application-Layer Delay Reduction Methods over Wireless Access Networks

Yoshiaki Nishikawa, Takashi Oshiba, Dai Kanetomo, and Kazuaki Nakajima

NEC Corporation, 1753 Shimonumabe, Nakahara-ku,
Kawasaki, Kanagawa, 211-8666 Japan
{y-nishikawa,nakajima}@ah.jp.nec.com, oshiba@cp.jp.nec.com,
d-kanetomo@ce.jp.nec.com

Abstract. In this paper, we discuss the experimental results of application-layer delay reduction methods, which can reduce the delay during TCP applications. Due to the popularization of smart phones, Wireless Local Area Network (WLAN) access such as WLAN hot spot or WLAN tethering is increasing. This increase leads to a WLAN channel being shared by multiple data flows, resulting in the degradation of the communication performance. Specifically, the delay of the real time applications that communicate over TCP can be made longer. To reduce the delay, we developed three methods: reducing the amount of data to send, triggering TCP's fast retransmission earlier, and returning TCP's acknowledgment immediately. In our experiments, we measured the delay during the real time TCP applications connected with each other over WLAN and commercial fixed network and analyzed the effectiveness of our methods in the case of WLAN performance being degraded by the file transfer flow. Results indicate that our methods can reduce the 95th percentile of the delay by as much as 84%.

Keywords: TCP, Delay Reduction, Application-Layer Method.

1 Introduction

Due to the popularization of smart phones, Wireless Local Area Network (WLAN) access is increasing. Internet access over WLAN is offered in various places such as homes, offices, and hotels. Mobile devices such as smart phones and tablets on which only wireless LAN is available have become popular. WLAN is thus being increasingly accessed by mobile devices in addition to PCs. It has also became common to access the Internet through mobile PCs, tablets, or gaming devices by using a mobile router or a WLAN tethering function on a smart phone. A mobile router is connected to the Internet via mobile wireless communication technology such as 3G and LTE and can function as a WLAN access point. The WLAN tethering involves using a smart phone as a mobile router. People are establishing their own WLAN on the basis of their demands and are connecting their mobile devices to the Internet.

M. Matera and G. Rossi (Eds.): MobiWIS 2013 Workshops, CCIS 183, pp. 17–24, 2013.

There are several problems degrading the performance of WLAN and real time applications. Competing and interfering problems occur because WLANs that do not cooperate with each other are established side by side. In the competing problem, the performance is degraded by the impact from other WLANs sharing the same communication channel. In contrast, in the interfering problem, the performance is degraded by the impact from other WLANs overlapping in the spectrum of the communication channel. There is also the problem of the growing traffic. More traffic is offloaded from mobile wireless systems to WLAN. These problems significantly affect the real time applications that communicate frequently over TCP because of its retransmission and reordering.

In this paper, we propose delay reduction methods on the real time applications and perform an experiment to evaluate these methods in the case of the performance of WLAN being degraded by the file transfer flow. We propose three methods: to reduce the number of data to send, to trigger the TCP fast retransmission earlier, and to return an ACK immediately. We try to reduce the delay to less than 100ms, which is required as the delay of a real time application [8]. Results show that our methods can reduce the 95th percentile of the delay by as much as 84% and meet the above requirement.

2 Related Work

In this section, we describe work related to this paper. Some researchers have sought ways to manage competing and interfering problems. Choi et al. proposed a channel selecting algorithm that scans channels used by other access points and selects its own channel automatically [3]. Lee et al. [2] proposed an approach to optimize access point placement and channel assignment in WLANs. Though these approaches to manage WLAN directly can improve WLAN performance, the cases in which we cannot manage WLAN ourselves need to be considered. Brosh et al. presented experimental results for the delay of a real time TCP application [4]. According to their paper, the method that splits data and uses multiple TCP connections can reduce the delay. In this paper, we evaluate our simple application-layer methods when the performance of WLAN is degraded by the file transfer flow.

3 Application

In this section, we explain the real time application we use. We use the Android device as a platform on which the application and our methods run. This is because Android devices are widely used to access to the Internet. For the real time application, we select an application that sends and receives a small size data that indicates user's operation on a touch panel. A remote desktop application is an example of this. We are interested in the End-to-End one way delay, which is the time that it takes data to travel across the network from source to destination. This is because the responsiveness of the real time application depends on how short the End-to-End delay is. For example, in a remote desktop application, a local device

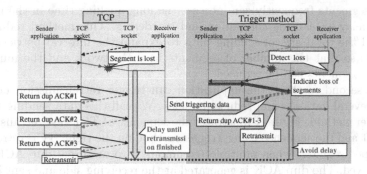

Fig. 1. Left: sequence of TCP fast retransmission. Right: sequence when Trigger method is used.

sends data indicating user's operation to a remote device and receives the result image from a remote device. The End-to-End delay of operation data becomes shorter, so users can obtain the result image earlier. Thus, the End-to-End delay of operation data must be reduced. In ITU-T Recommendation Y.1541 [8], 100ms is required as the End-to-End one way delay of a real time application. Hereinafter, we refer to the delay as the End-to-End one way delay.

We suppose that two of TCP's controls make the delay long. One is the reordering control to reconstruct the sending order on the receiving side. TCP performs the retransmission when it detects a loss of a segment. Throughout this paper, we refer to the transmission unit of TCP as a segment and to the transmission unit of application as data. By the reordering control, the segment sent after the dropped segment is waited for at the buffer of the receiving side until the lost segment has been transmitted safely. Then, the delays of data corresponding to the waited segments are extended. More data are delayed by the reordering control in the real time application than in the non-real time application that sends data less frequently. Second is the flow control to avoid the buffer overflow at the receiving side. TCP limits the number of segments that TCP can send without receiving ACK. After reaching the limit, TCP delays sending till receiving ACK at the sending side. At the receiving side, TCP also delays returning ACK until the timer have reached a certain timeout value or the receiver has received multiple segments. While TCP delays returning ACK, the number of segments that have been sent already by the sending side is more likely to reach the limit in the real time application than in the non-real time application.

4 Methods

In this section, we propose three delay reduction methods on the real time applications. In the first method, the application can reduce the number of data to send and its consumption of bandwidth. We call this data reducing method the Reduction-P method, where P is the factor representing reduction percentage.

Sending segments frequently can increase the long queuing time in the network and the delay by causing congestion and reordering. This method reduces the times and the total size of sending data to expand the interval between sending events so that the number of segments in the network and the number of congested segments can be reduced.

In the second method, the application can trigger retransmission faster by sending several datasets and reduce its delay. We call this data sending method the Trigger method. Figure 1 illustrates the sequence of TCP fast retransmission on the left and the sequence using Trigger method on the right. TCP retransmits the dropped segment when multiple (commonly two or three) dup ACKs have been received. The dup ACK is generated at the receiving side and sent in reply to the sending side when the segment is received in the wrong order. In Trigger method, the receiver infers the loss of segments from the interval of receiving data that is too long. Then the receiver sends the data indicating the loss of segments. Immediately after receiving this data, the sender sends the certain number of the triggering data that are very few. When these triggering data are received at the receiver side, dup ACKs corresponding to the triggering data is sent in reply to the sender. Then at the sending side, the dropped segment is retransmitted since a certain number of dup ACK has been received.

In the third method, the application can sending TCP ACK in reply immediately by returning data even though Delayed ACK is enabled. We call this method the Return method. TCP delays sending ACK in reply as we mentioned before. TCP has the piggyback ACK function in which ACK can be sent in reply when there is a segment to be sent at the receiver side. In the Return method, the receiver sends data in replay immediately after receiving data to send ACK in replay immediately.

5   Experimental Setup

In this section, we explain the experimental environment and settings. Figure 2 shows the experiment network we used. The network consists of three home networks illustrated in the left of the figure and one server's network illustrated in the bottom right. These four networks are connected with each other over the commercial fixed network via FTTH. The sender application runs on the Android device in the sender's network. Two receiver applications run on the Android device in both two receiversf networks. Two receiversf networks have different Received Signal Strength Indication (RSSI). The higher one is −40 dBm, and the lower is −58 dBm. Android devices are connected to wireless access points over IEEE802.11n. In the server's network, the relay server is connected to the wired router. The sender application sends data to the relay server, and the relay server relays the data to one of the receiver applications. Our methods are controlled between the sender application-to-relay server and relay server-to-receiver application. To simulate the degradation of the WLAN performance, Windows PC is used, which is the same model to the relay server connected to the access point over IEEE802.11n in the sender's network and can make

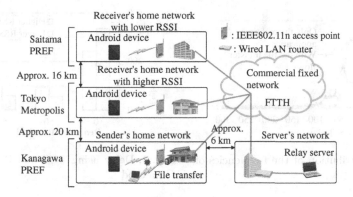

Fig. 2. The experiment network

Table 1. Device specification

	Android device	Relay server
Product name	SGH-N023[6]	VY14AC-W[7]
OS	Android OS 2.3	Windows XP SP3
CPU	S5PC110 1GHz	core2duo 1.4GHz
RAM	0.51 GB	2.96 GB
NIC	Wireless (IEEE802.11n)	Wired (1000BASE-T)

bulk file transfer flow from network attached storage in the same WLAN. The specifications of the Android device and relay server are shown in Table 1. We use AtermWR8750N as an WLAN access point and wired router. Its available bandwidth is about 184 Mbps as an wireless access point and about 840 Mbps as a wired router [5].

In our experiment, we use the data generated sequentially by sliding a finger on the touch panel as the data communicated between applications. These data are sent at 60 times by each 30ms. Each piece of data is 50 bytes and is sent immediately from application to TCP. Like most delay sensitive applications, Nagle's algorithm [1] is disabled in this paper. We refer to the stream as the data generated by one sliding event and the delay of a stream as the delay calculated by the average of the delay of data of which one stream consists. In the following part of this paper, we describe the delay of the stream, not the delay of each piece of data. The delay of the real time application needs to be less than 100ms[8]. Our goal is to fulfill this requirement. Statistics typically used to evaluate the delay are mean, median, or mode averages. To evaluate the delay sensitive real time application, these statistics are not considered appropriate. This is because the long delay that does occur not very often spoils the real time application. Thus, we use the 95th percentile, which is the most commonly used percentile value.

We measured to ensure that the file transfer flow degrades the performance of WLAN. Figure 3 shows the distribution of the frequencies of the delay of all 300 streams measured in the two cases: with or without a file transfer flow.

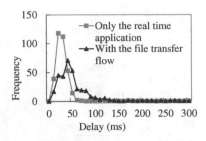
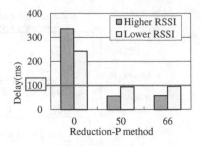

Fig. 3. Distribution of the frequencies of the delay

Fig. 4. Delay using TCP and Reduction-P method

This distribution is drawn with the delay of the stream on the abscissa axis and the frequencies of the delay on the ordinate. We can see that the delay in the case with the file transfer flow is longer than that in the case of only the real time application flow. In the case of only the real time application flow, the maximum delay is 162ms and the 95th percentile of the delay is 42ms. In the case with the file transfer flow, the maximum delay is 2451ms, which is not displayed, and the 95th percentile of the delay is 354ms. Thus, the performance of WLAN is clearly degraded due to the file transfer flow.

In our experiment, each of our methods is set as follows. In the Reduction-P method, P is set to 50 or 66. Intervals are expanded from 30ms to 60ms or 90ms, respectively. In the Trigger method, we set the time used by the receiver to infer the loss of segments to the time made by adding the interval decided by the Reduction-P method and 20ms. For the Return method, we tested with and without the Return method.

6　Experimental Results

In this section, we show experimental results of each method compared with results of TCP. Then, we show results of combinations of our methods. In the following section, we refer to the 95th delay as the 95th percentile of the delay, and figures are drawn with the name of methods on the abscissa axis and the 95th delay on the ordinate. Each 95th delay in this section is calculated by delays of 300 streams.

Figure 4 shows the 95th delay when using TCP and the Reduction-P method with higher RSSI and lower RSSI. In the case with higher RSSI, the 95th delay by using TCP is 336ms, and the delays by using Reduction-50 and Reduction-33 are 56ms and 58ms, respectively. In the case with lower RSSI, the 95th delay by using TCP is 242ms, and the delays by reducing the number of data to 30 and 20 are 95ms and 98ms, respectively. By reducing the number of data to 30, the delay is reduced by 83%. This is despite there being just a marginal difference between 30 and 20 as the number of data. Figure 5 shows the 95th delay when using TCP and the Trigger method with higher RSSI and lower RSSI. In the case with higher RSSI, the 95th delay by using the Trigger method is 96ms and is reduced by 73% compared with the delay by using TCP. In the case with lower

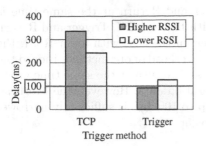

Fig. 5. Delay when using TCP and Trigger method

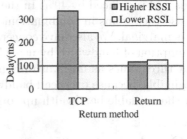

Fig. 6. Delay when using TCP and Return method

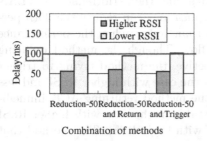

Fig. 7. Delay when using only Reduction-50, by Reduction-50 with Trigger and Reduction-50 with Return

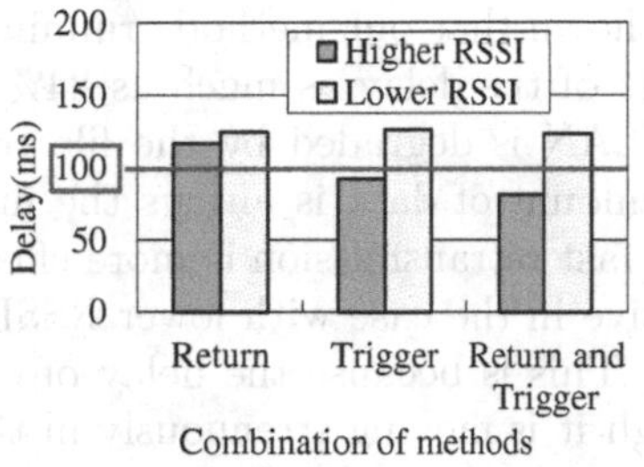

Fig. 8. Delay when using only Trigger, by only Return and Trigger with Return

RSSI, the 95th delay by using the Trigger method is 126ms and is reduced by 48%. Figure 6 shows the 95th delay when using TCP and the Return method with higher RSSI and lower RSSI. In the case with higher RSSI, the 95th delay by using the Return method is 116ms and is reduced by 65% compared with the delay using TCP. In the case with lower RSSI, the 95th delay by using the Return method is 124ms and is reduced by 49%.

Figure 7 shows the 95th delay with higher RSSI and lower RSSI by using only Reduction-50, Reduction-50 with Trigger, and Reduction-50 with Return. In the case with higher RSSI, the 95th delays by using Reduction-50 with Trigger and with Return are 55ms and 60ms, respectively, and are reduced by as much as 84% compared with the delay using TCP. In the case with lower RSSI, the 95th delays by using Reduction-50 with Trigger and with Return are 101ms and 94ms, respectively, and are reduced by as much as 61%. Reduction-50 method does not need to be combined with other methods. In the case with higher RSSI, Reduction-50 and Return decrease their gains in combination. In the case with lower RSSI, Reduction-50 and Trigger decrease their gains too.

Figure 8 shows the 95th delay with higher RSSI and lower RSSI when using only the Trigger method, only the Return method, and the Trigger method with the Return method. In the case with higher RSSI, the 95th delay by using Trigger and Return at the same time is 81ms and is reduced by 76%. In the case with lower RSSI, the 95th delay by using Trigger and Return at the same time is 123ms and is reduced by 49%. In the case with higher RSSI, Trigger and Return increase their gains in combination. However, in the case with lower RSSI, the gain is marginal. We also have concern about overhead of our method. Indeed the consumption of bandwidth by using Trigger and Return at the same time grows about three times as much as only user operation data. However, the overhead is negligible, because overhead bandwidth up to 100kbps is sufficiently narrower than the available bandwidth up to 180Mbps[5].

7 Conclusion

We have ensured that the file transfer flow degrades the performance of WLAN and shown that our methods running on applications can reduce the 95th percentile of the delay as much as 84% to less than 100ms when the performance of WLAN is degraded by the file transfer flow. Though the method reducing the amount of data is always the most effective, the method trying to trigger TCP fast retransmission is more effective in the case with higher RSSI and less effective in the case with lower RSSI than the method returning ACK immediately. This is because the delay of data is stable in the case with higher RSSI though it is moving strenuously in the case with lower RSSI. The method that tries to trigger the TCP fast retransmission earlier can reduce the delay due to losses of segments, which does not happen very often in the case with higher RSSI. However, this method is not very effective due to the fixed timer when the delay is changing strenuously. Therefore, the method that tries to return ACK immediately is more effective in the case with lower RSSI.

References

1. Nagle, J.: Congestion Control in IP/TCP Internetworks. RFC 896 (January 1984)
2. Lee, Y., Kim, K., Choi, Y.: Optimization of AP Placement and Channel Assignment in Wireless LANs. In: Proceedings of the 27th Annual IEEE Conference on Local Computer Networks, LCN 2002, November 6-8 (2002)
3. Choi, J., Lee, K., Lee, S.R., Ihm, J.(J.): Channel Selection for IEEE 802.11 Based Wireless LANs Using 2.4GHz Band. IEICE Electronics Express (ELEX) 8(16), 1275–1280 (2011, 2012)
4. Brosh, E., Baset, S.A., Rubenstein, D., Schulzrinne, H.: The Delay-Friendliness of TCP. In: SIGMETRICS (June 2008)
5. NEC Corporation. Product Information of AtermWR8750N, http://121ware.com/product/atermstation/product/warpstar/wr8750n-hp/
6. SAMSUNG. Product Information of GALAXY Tab SC-01C, http://www.samsung.com/jp/support/model/SGH-N023CWNDCM
7. NEC Corporation. Product Information of VersaPro, http://121ware.com/e-manual/m/nx/vp/base/vy14acw.html
8. ITU-T Recommendation Y.1541: Network performance objectives for IP-based services (2011)

Embedded Data on Intelligent
Products – Impact on Real-Time Applications

Sylvain Kubler[1,*], William Derigent[2], Éric Rondeau[2],
André Thomas[2], and Kary Främling[1]

[1] Aalto University, School of Science, Espoo, Finland
P.O. Box 15400, FI-00076 Aalto, Finland
[2] Université de Lorraine, CRAN, UMR 7039, Vandœuvre-lès-Nancy, F-54506, France
CNRS, CRAN, UMR 7039, Vandœuvre lès Nancy, F-54506, France
sylvain.kubler@aalto.fi

Abstract. New challenges and opportunities arise with the Internet of
Things (IoT), making it possible to link any objects of the real world with
the virtual one. In recent years, IoT has become increasingly popular
in industrial applications (e.g. for the inclusion of data related to the
product history). It might therefore be asked what is the impact on
real-time applications when accessing data from the object instead of
accessing it from the database. To assess that impact, this paper develops
an approach that uses jointly two simulators: CPN Tools® and OPNET
Modeler®. This approach is then applied on a benchmark scenario.

Keywords: Internet of Things, Intelligent product, Real-time system,
Data dissemination, Product life cycle.

1 Introduction

Today, the study of the product life cycle (PLC) is an integral part of the company strategy to plan, design and manage the life of their products more effectively. In general, the PLC consists of three main phases as depicted in Fig. 1:
Beginning of Life (BoL), Middle of Life (MoL) and End of Life (EoL). The different applications and actors from the PLC require specific product-related data
to fulfill their mission (e.g. production orders, maintenance orders, traceability
data) [1,2]. Product-related data is of great importance since it is all that people
can work with when the product does not physically exist in their environment.
Making product-related data sharable among all actors of the PLC is a major
challenge [3].

With the advance of new technologies (nanotechnology, RFID, cloud computing), objects of the real world can be linked with the virtual one, thus enabling
connectivity anywhere, anytime and for anything [4]. Such objects are also referred to as "smart" or "intelligent products", and are the essence of concepts as
ubiquitous/pervasive computing and Internet of Things (IoT). These concepts

---

* Corresponding author.

M. Matera and G. Rossi (Eds.): MobiWIS 2013 Workshops, CCIS 183, pp. 25–34, 2013.

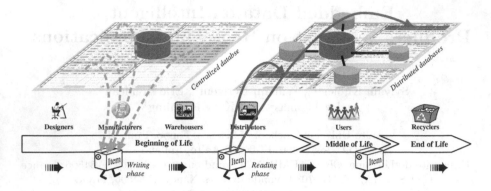

Fig. 1. Illustration of a *writing* and *reading* operation of the product during the PLC

refer to a world where physical objects and beings, as well as virtual data and environments, all interact with each other in the same space and time [5]. It can be stated that, today, IoT applications are mainly defined in MoL (smart house, smart space,...) but become increasingly popular in BoL and EoL [6]. For instance, much research work has been carried out in that direction by the IMS (Intelligent Manufacturing System) community over the last decade, which promotes the use of intelligent products to make systems more efficient and flexible [2]. Several definitions and classifications of an "intelligent product" are admitted, but the common denominator is that the product should be able to communicate effectively with its environment and should be able to optimize its operations, usage and other behavior. Meyer et al. [7] provide a comprehensive survey on intelligent products and related applications. Among their statements, the authors reveal that intelligent products often only provide a network pointer (e.g. via a RFID tag) to a linked database and a decision making software agent. However, in recent years, it is not uncommon to see products with larger data-storage capacities with faster data writing and reading [8,9].

Since products can carry more data than old ID technologies, it is quite natural to store, at important stages of the PLC, a subset of useful data from some databases onto the product as illustrated in Fig. 1 (*cf. Writing phase*). Therefore, this data is always available with the object to which it is attached, regardless of the network availability, and it could be retrieved in any other upstream PLC stages (*cf. Reading phase* in Fig. 1). For instance, Suzuki et al. [10] explain that intelligent products are used in the airline industry for the inclusion of aircraft part history records, which may be very useful in maintenance operations. In line with this work, some scholars developed approaches aiming at selecting the most appropriate subset of data for its inclusion onto the product [9,11]. These approaches are particularly interesting because they take into account the context of use of the data and the product (user's expectations, geographic location of the product,...) for such a data selection. However, to the best of our knowledge, no work has yet studied the impact on real-time performance when accessing data from the product instead of accessing it from the database.

This paper proposes a preliminary study to assess such an impact. In our context, the product undergoes different operations through its PLC and each operator requires particular data fragments (i.e. information subsets) to fulfill his/its mission. These data fragments are assumed to be stored/accessed either from a database or from the product itself (e.g. a product fitted with a RFID tag), assuming that both devices are always available in the application. Based on this approach, it is then possible to assess each data access schema from a time perspective. Petri Net models (using CPN Tools) are used for modeling the sequence of operations undergone by the product, used together with the OPNET Modeler for taking into account realistic time behaviors for accessing data considering a specific communication network. This approach is described in section 2, and is then applied on a benchmark scenario in section 3. This proposal could further be used as a criterion for selecting the appropriate information to be stored on the product, at different stages of the PLC. For instance, in [9], this appropriateness is based on a degree of data relevance computed by taking into account several criteria. These criteria reflect the context of use of the product (actor's expectations, product's location,...), and new ones may be defined in this approach (e.g. a criterion reflecting the impact on the time when accessing data from the product instead of accessing it from the database).

2 Assessment Approach of Real-Time Impact

2.1 Scenario Modeling Using Petri Nets and Network Simulations

In this study, Petri Nets are used for modeling, simulating, and analyzing the sequence of operations undergone by the product (i.e. the operations to be assessed). Petri Net model is designed by working on hierarchical views, thus facilitating the sequence modeling. For instance, the upper view could model the considered operation sequence as depicted in Fig. 2 (the upper view denoted view 0) , while the bottom views (view 1, 2,...) could model the characteristics of each operation like the operation duration, the set of data fragments required for achieving the operation, the resource assignment (e.g. arrival frequency of the products, size of the product queue), as depicted through the zoom made on operation 4 (denoted view 1).

The second simulator - OPNET is primarily aimed at developing and analyzing communication networks, devices, protocols and applications. It is used in our study to model and simulate the network architecture[1], thus making it possible to estimate the times to perform read/write queries on/from a database and on/from a product. These times are referred to as Round Trip Times[2] (RTTs).

---

[1] OPNET Modeler offers a wide selection of technologies and devices, but also provides a programming platform to develop new communication models. For instance, Dongkai and Wenli [12] designed the RFID reader models and tag models according to the EPCglobal Class-1 Generation-2 Protocol.

[2] *Round Trip Time*: time between sending the first packet of a query and receiving the last packet of the response.

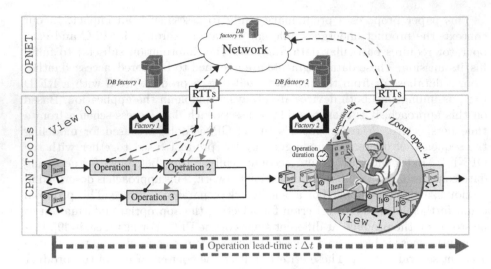

Fig. 2. Assessment approach using jointly two simulators: CPN tools & OPNET

RTTs are then injected/added in the Petri Net as symbolized by the dashed arrows in Fig. 2. More concretely, RTTs are bounded to Petri Net transitions, which represent the action of performing queries.

2.2 Real-Time Impact Assessment

Based on Petri Net simulations, the objective is then to compare different data access schemas, where a data fragment could be either accessed from the database system or from the product. One possibility of data access schema is defined via n boolean values [F1, F2,..., Fn], with n the total number of data fragments:

- Fk means that the data fragment k is accessed from the product,
- $\overline{Fk}$ means that the data fragment k is accessed from the database,

For instance, [$\overline{F1}$, $\overline{F2}$,..., Fn] informs the simulator that Fn is accessed from the product and F1, F2 from the database. In total, 2^n data access schemas are simulated and compared. The comparison is based on the time to complete the operation sequence, noted "operation lead-time" Δt in Fig. 3, which inevitably varies according to the data access schema.

3   Applicative Scenario

Three operations composing a PLC are defined in this scenario, which are modeled and assessed in term of real-time performance. These three operations are modeled via CPN Tools as depicted[3] in Fig. 3, where each operator requires specific data to complete his/its tasks. In this scenario, an operation is considered

---

[3] Only view 0 of the hierarchical views is presented, but three levels have been defined in total in order to characterize all operation features (as explained in section 2.1).

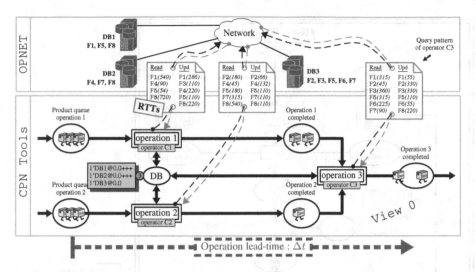

Fig. 3. View 0 of the Petri Net hierarchy: operation sequencing in the PLC

as completed once all data fragments required by the operator have been accessed/updated, and once the operation duration is ended. As a result, the time to fulfill the operation is somehow dependent on the RTTs, which are estimated via OPNET simulations based on a specific network architecture and operator's query pattern (i.e. a set of read/write query performed by each operator).

In that regard and to make the paper even more interesting, an optimal data distribution is considered as a benchmark. This benchmark is the one from [13], where a scenario considering 3 databases (DB1 to DB3), 3 clients/operators (C1 to C3) and 8 data fragments (F1 to F8) is defined. These data fragments are accessed by each operator according to a specific query pattern, and are accordingly distributed (optimally) over the 3 databases. Fig. 3 shows each operator's query pattern (the number in brackets indicating the number of bytes read/written) and the resulting data fragment allocation (F1, F5, F8 allocated to DB1, *etc.*). The network architecture, the data distribution and the operator's query patterns are configured in OPNET[4]. The RTT of each query (performed by each operator) is then estimated from OPNET simulations and injected in the appropriate Petri Net view, as symbolized by the dashed arrows in Fig. 3. By way of indication[5], the operator C3 spends $\simeq 5ms$ for reading 45 bytes of F2 and $\simeq 12ms$ for writing 330 bytes of F2. Fig. 4 shows the Petri Net model that defines the sequencing of operation 1 (i.e. the transition denoted **operation 1** in

---

[4] The exact network architecture is given in Fig. 5, which shows that data can be either accessed from DB1, DB2, DB3 or from the product. For information purposes, the following equipments have been used in simulations: routers *Cisco 1600*, switches *Cisco 2900XL*, server *Sun Ultra* 10 333*Mhz*::1 *CPU*, 1 *Core per CPU, Solaris*.

[5] RTTs depend on various parameters such as the hardware, the technique of data replication implemented (synchronous, asynchronous), *etc.* Due to the space limitations, all parameters are not presented.

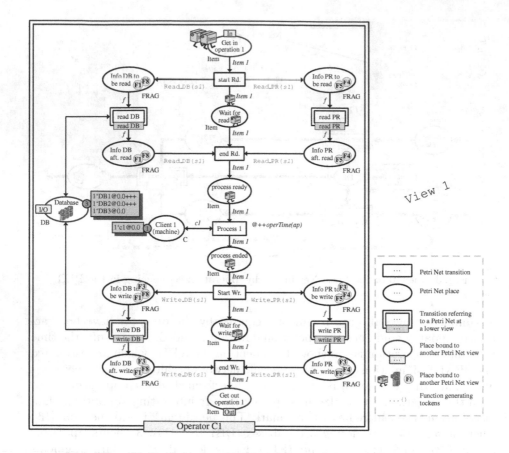

Fig. 4. Toto

view 0/Fig. 3). This Petri Net thus corresponds to a view 1 (i.e. a lower view to view 0). Two other views 1 (not detailed in this paper) are also defined regarding the transitions operation 2 and operation 3 of view 0. In Fig. 4, when a product arrives in the queue for being processed (i.e. in the place named Get in operation 1[6]), the set of data fragments that must be read by Client 1 (i.e. F1, F4, F5, F8; *cf.* Fig. 3) are immediately generated by the functions fd1R_DB(*sc1*) and fd1R_P(*sc1*), with *sc1* the data access schema. In other words, *sc1* indicates if the data fragment Fi ($i \in \{1,..,8\}$) is read from the database (in such a case, a color token is generated in the place denoted Info DB to be read) or from the product (the token is generated in the place denoted Info PR to be read). In the example given in Fig. 4, *sc1* specifies that F1, F8 are read from the database, while F4, F5 from the product. Once all data fragments have been read (i.e. once

---

[6] Get in operation 1 is a place linked with the upper view (view 0). Likewise, places Database and Get out operation 1 in Fig. 4 are respectively I/O (Input/Output) and O (Output) of this Petri Net/view.

transactions **read DB** and **read PR** are crossed[7]), products are then ready to be processed by Client 1 (see place **process ready**). Transition **Process 1** represents such a process with $@++operTime(item1)$ the function that binds the time required to process the product to the transition. Once **process 1** is completed, data fragments are updated in a similar way than before, whether they are accessed from the database or from the product (see the places named **Info DB to be write** and **Info PR to be write**). Finally, products are added to the place denoted **Get out operation 1** before moving towards operation 3 (*cf.* Fig. 3).

2^8 (i.e. 256) data access schemas are simulated with CPN Tools and the resulting operation lead-times Δt are recorded (*cf.* Fig. 3). In our scenario, there are 8 data access schemas considering all possibilities of accessing one data fragment from the product (see Table 1); 28 schemas when accessing two data fragments from the product, and so on. Sections 3.1 and 3.2 present and compare the operation lead-times resulting from simulations, when using respectively a reliable network and a network with traffic overload.

Table 1. Possibilities of data access schemas considering 8 data fragments

	Solution	Detailed Solution		Solution	Detailed Solution
	1	[F1 F2 F3 F4 F5 F6 F7 **F8**]		1	[F1 F2 F3 F4 F5 F6 **F7 F8**]
	2	[F1 F2 F3 F4 F5 F6 **F7** F8]		2	[F1 F2 F3 F4 F5 **F6** F7 **F8**]
1/8 fragment on the product	3	[F1 F2 F3 F4 F5 **F6** F7 F8]	2/8 fragment on the product	3	[F1 F2 F3 F4 **F5** F6 F7 **F8**]
	4	[F1 F2 F3 F4 **F5** F6 F7 F8]		:	:
	5	[F1 F2 F3 **F4** F5 F6 F7 F8]		:	:
	6	[F1 F2 **F3** F4 F5 F6 F7 F8]		26	[**F1** F2 F3 **F4** F5 F6 F7 F8]
	7	[F1 **F2** F3 F4 F5 F6 F7 F8]		27	[**F1** F2 **F3** F4 F5 F6 F7 F8]
	8	[**F1** F2 F3 F4 F5 F6 F7 F8]		28	[**F1 F2** F3 F4 F5 F6 F7 F8]

3.1 Reliable Network

In our experiments, two product throughputs (i.e. the transmit rate of the wireless communication between the product and the wired network) are defined: 1Mb/s (high-speed RFID technology) and 11Mb/s (802.11b standard). The operation lead-times Δt resulting from the 256 simulations, considering both product throughputs, are synthesized in a box and whisker diagram in Fig. 5. It gives the min, the 1st-3th quartile, the median and the max Δt (see the y-axis) resulting to the different possibilities for accessing 0 data fragment out of 8 from the product (0/8 in Fig. 5; i.e. all data fragments are accessed from the database only), 1 data fragment out of 8 from the product (1/8; i.e. 7 data fragments are accessed from the database only), and so on. The data access schema 0/8 indicates it took 2'30" (Δt) to complete the three operations[8]. The data access

---

[7] RTTs estimated from OPNET are injected in a lower view (view 2), which represents the step sequencing of the transaction **read DB** of Fig. 4/view 1.

[8] The product throughput does not have any impact on Δt since no data is accessed from the product.

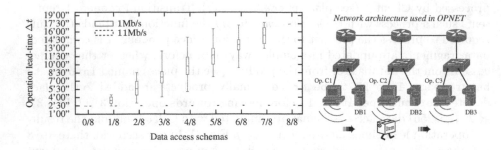

Fig. 5. Impact on times when accessing data from the product: reliable network

schema 1/8, with a product throughput of 1Mb/s, indicates that one possibility among the 8 data access schemas listed in Table 1 (*cf.* table "1 fragment from the product") requires 2′30″ to complete the three operations (*cf.* the min Δt value), while another possibility out of the 8 requires 4′45″ (*cf.* the max Δt value). More generally, it can be observed in this scenario that it is always faster to access data from the database considering a product throughput of 1Mb/s ($2′30″ \leq \Delta t \leq 17′30″$). However, in the case where products communicate at 11Mb/s, all solutions are identical (i.e. 2′30″). In conclusion, there is no point to store/access data fragments on the product since the database is always a better or an equivalent solution.

3.2 Overload Network Situation

A traffic is added to the network between PC1 and PC2 as shown in Fig. 6 (PC1 sends 1500bytes/s to PC2). This overload inevitably generates delays on queries intended for, or originating from DB1. In such a situation, the whisker diagram in Fig. 6 shows that gains on Δt are obtained with the two product throughputs. In case of 11Mb/s, the higher the number of data fragments accessed from the product, the lesser Δt. In case of 1Mb/s, this statement is true until 3/8 because the three max Δt are always lower than 12′30″, which is Δt at 0/8. However, when accessing more than 3 data fragments from the product, Δt therefore becomes higher and higher (*cf.* the median and max values), exceeding 12′30″, even reaching 18′00″.

Based on this study, it can be concluded that in such a situation, it is better to access the 8 data fragments from the product when they communicate at 11Mb/s. However, in case where they communicate at 1Mb/s, the solution providing the smallest Δt is a data access schema 3/8, which precisely corresponds to the following schema: [$\overline{F1}$ $\overline{F2}$ **F3** $\overline{F4}$ $\overline{F5}$ **F6** **F7** $\overline{F8}$], as emphasized in Fig. 6.

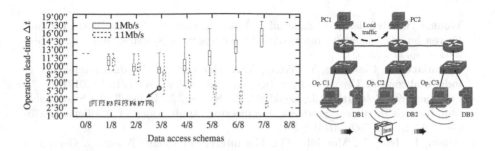

Fig. 6. Impact on times when accessing data from the product: overload traffic

4 Conclusion

Objects and products are increasingly being fitted with new technologies (RFID, sensors) that can store increasing quantities of data about themselves. In the context of product life cycle, it is a formidable challenge to link product-related data to the products themselves, thus making the information easily achievable throughout their life. However, to the best of our knowledge, no work has yet studied the impact on real-time performance about accessing data from the product instead of accessing it from the database system. Accordingly, this paper develops an approach to assess such an impact, which enables to determine in which situation(s) it is beneficial (from a time perspective) to access data from the product. A scenario is then proposed and shows that the impact on real-time strongly depends on the application features (product throughput, network state).

Results show that accessing to all information from the database does not penalize the application considering temporal aspects, unlike accessing it from the product/object. However, in situations where e.g. network disruptions occurs, results show that the application performance can be improved. In current work, Taguchi experiments are carried out to identify which factors mainly impact on the application performance (is it the data access schema? the arrival frequency of the products? the size of the product queue?...), and what is their degree of impact. These factors could further be used as a criterion for selecting the appropriate information to be stored on the product, at different stages of the PLC. For instance, in [9], the degree of data relevance is computed based on several criteria (actor's expectations, product's location,...), where new ones could be defined (e.g. a criterion reflecting the impact on the time when accessing data from the product instead of accessing it from the database).

Acknowledgement. This work is supported by OPNET via "Teaching with OPNET" program. The authors gratefully acknowledge the financial support of the CPER 2007-2013.

References

1. Wong, C.Y., Mcfarlane, D., Zaharudin, A.A., Agarwal, V.: The Intelligent Product Driven Supply Chain. In: International Conference on Systems, Man and Cybernetics, pp. 4–6 (2002)
2. McFarlane, D., Giannikas, V., Wong, A.C., Harrison, M.: Product intelligence in industrial control: Theory and practice. Annual Reviews in Control (2013)
3. Främling, K., Holmström, J., Loukkola, J., Nyman, J., Kaustell, A.: Sustainable plm through intelligent products. Engineering Applications of Artificial Intelligence 26(2), 789–799 (2013)
4. Atzori, L., Iera, A., Morabito, G.: The internet of things: A survey. Computer Networks 54(15), 2787–2805 (2010)
5. Sundmaeker, H., Guillemin, P., Friess, P., Woelfflé, S.: Vision and challenges for realising the Internet of Things. Cluster of European Research Projects on the Internet of Things, European Commision (2010)
6. Kiritsis, D.: Closed-loop plm for intelligent products in the era of the internet of things. Computer-Aided Design 43(5), 479–501 (2011)
7. Meyer, G., Främling, K., Holmström, J.: Intelligent products: A survey. Computers in Industry 60(3), 137–148 (2009)
8. Jun, H.B., Suh, H.W.: Decision on the memory size of embedded information systems in an ubiquitous maintenance environment. Computers & Industrial Engineering 56(1), 444–451 (2009)
9. Kubler, S., Derigent, W., Thomas, A., Rondeau, E.: Embedding data on "communicating materials" from context-sensitive information analysis. Journal of Intelligent Manufacturing (2013), doi:10.1007/s10845-013-0745-y
10. Suzuki, S., Harrison, M.: Data synchronization specification. aerospace-id program report. Technical report, Auto-ID Labs, University of Cambridge (2006)
11. Chan, D., Roddick, J.: Context-sensitive mobile database summarisation. In: 26th Australasian Computer Science Conference, vol. 16, pp. 139–149 (2003)
12. Dongkai, Y., Wenli, L.: The wireless channel modeling for rfid system with opnet. In: Proceedings of the 5th International Conference on Wireless Communications, Networking and Mobile Computing, pp. 3803–3805 (2009)
13. Hababeh, I., Bowring, N., Ramachandran, M.: A method for fragment allocation design in the distributed database systems. In: The 6th Annual UAE University Research Conference (2005)

Accessibility of Mobile Web Apps by Screen Readers of Touch-Based Mobile Phones

Afnan A. Al-Subaihin[1], Atheer S. Al-Khalifa[2], and Hend S. Al-Khalifa[1]

[1] Information Technology Department, King Saud University,
{aalSubaihin,hendk}@ksu.edu.sa
[2] Computer Research Institute, King AbdulAziz City for Science and Technology,
Riyadh, Saudi Arabia
aalkhalifa@kacst.edu.sa

Abstract. Current mobile web applications (apps) can be accessed using a mobile browser through a URL, or, packaged using specific packaging tools and libraries as native apps. To access these apps, Visually Impaired People (VIP) relay on screen readers that come built-in with smart phones. Among the well-known mobile phones' screen readers is VoiceOver by Apple. In this paper we discuss the results of testing the accessibility of mobile web apps via Voice-Over and observe its performance. As a result of this observation we suggest some basic guidelines for designing mobile web apps.

Keywords: Mobile accessibility, Mobile Web Apps, screen reader, Touch-Based Mobile Phones, blind users, VoiceOver.

1   Introduction

Nowadays, the World Wide Web plays a central and significant role in facilitating communication, education, entertainment, industry and government transactions. It is also regarded as an unlimited source of information.

Providing global access to the many services hosted by the World Wide Web is considered as a basic human right regardless of someone's impairment. This accessibility issue is taken to a new paradigm as Smartphone usage continues to grow; making mobile phones one of the most platforms used to access the web and benefit from its features.

As mobile web apps are built using the collaboration of markup languages to identify page structure, Style Sheets for aesthetic elements including positioning of page components and scripting languages to provide event driven interaction, all these components should homogeneously produce an application that adheres to accessibility standards. However, this does not ensure the capability of mobile screen readers to fully enable accessibility of the mobile web app for Visually Impaired People (VIP), since it depends on the collaboration of developer's code, the screen reader itself and the web browser.

Mobile web apps are accessed via mobile phones using two distinctive methods. Either they are hosted on a web server and thus accessible using a mobile browser

M. Matera and G. Rossi (Eds.): MobiWIS 2013 Workshops, CCIS 183, pp. 35–43, 2013.

through a URL. Alternatively, mobile web apps can be packaged using specific packaging tools and libraries as native apps; hence, they can be deployed as native apps in the mobile vendor's application store. This kind of app runs natively on the operating system, however, the underlying code remains a web code.

In this paper, we evaluate a very common mobile screen reader which is Voice-Over and analyze its shortcomings and the difficulties encountered due to the touch nature of the mobile phone when dealing with mobile web apps. We also discuss the source of these shortcomings and ways to avoid them. The aim of this evaluation is to come up with an initial list of guidelines and recommendations for web developers to maximize their applications' accessibility whether the application is web hosted or packaged as a native app.

The rest of the paper is organized as follows: section 2 gives a brief background about mobile screen readers, browsers and apps. Section 3 presents some related work in the field of screen readers' evaluations. Section 4 shows the methodology used to setup and test mobile web apps. Section 5 discusses the results of the evaluation. Finally section 6 concludes the paper with lessons learned and design guidelines.

2   Background

In this section we will highlight two important technologies, namely: mobile screen readers and browsers.

2.1   Mobile Screen Readers

Screen readers are software programs that can be installed on a blind's computer or mobile to convert visual information into audible description; enabling the user to navigate through interfaces using shortcut keys or gestures. The spoken information produced by these programs is a result of a Text To Speech (TTS) engine that is integrated with the screen reader. It also allows the user to perform different essential tasks: reading and editing documents, browsing the web, managing files, etc. [1].

Apple^{TM} devices, for example, feature a built-in screen reader called VoiceOver^{TM} along with other technologies that provide assistance for VIP. Whereas Google Android^{TM} has TalkBack^{TM} service pre-installed to its system with similar functionality.

VoiceOver is the built-in screen reader for Mac OS and it is also included in the mobile version of the system. It can be activated through the Settings menu or by pressing the Home button three times successively (if this feature is enabled) to turn it on or off.

Since new mobile phones incorporate an advanced touch screen as its main and only input method, the screen reader is designed to be controlled using a set of touch gestures. When enabled, the set of gestures for the device changes where a single tap focuses on an item speaking its name and double tap would launch the associated action [2].

2.2   Web Browsers and Web Apps

A web browser is one of the most important applications on mobiles. Fortunately with newer browsers following W3C newer standards e.g. HTML5/CSS3 and using cross-platform technologies e.g. JQuery/JavaScript, the mobile browsers domain has become less fragmented. Moreover, different mobile platforms' browsers are based on the open source web browser engine: Web-kit [3] e.g. Chrome, Safari (except of Windows 7 phone, which is IE 7 based).

Mobile web apps take advantage of mobile browsers' support and web technologies standardization to implement a website that can be deployed across various devices. These apps are developed using HTML, CSS and JavaScript technologies. Some frame-works enables developers to build mobile websites and/or port existing web-sites to a mobile friendly version e.g. Mobilize.js . While others offer native user interface elements such as tabs and views, and enable interaction to some hardware features such as mobile camera and storage system, e.g. Titanium Mobile. Moreover some frameworks are capable of packaging the apps with specific engines to enable them to be installed, accessed offline and distributed through market stores e.g. PhoneGap (http://phonegap.com/).

3   Related Work

Much of the research up to now has focused on desktop screen readers' evaluation of complete websites. For instance, Sandhya and Devi [4] investigated the accessibility of AJAX technology and JAWS screen reader then suggested few best practices for AJAX accessibility along with general approaches for designing accessible websites. Another suite of research lead by Maria Claudia Buzzi inspected accessibility of different types of web applications such as Google Docs [5], e-Learning systems [6] and eBay [7]. Also screen readers' performance with web applications in other languages were tested e.g. the "Big Eye" Chinese Screen Reader [8].

While desktop screen readers had their fair share of testing and evaluation in the research community, we have noticed a relatively low amount of literature regarding mobile screen readers' evaluation. Leporini et al. [9] investigated usability and accessibility issues in interactions with mobiles using VoiceOver. The study was conducted through remote inspection of VoiceOver and its gestures interactions with selected apps in the devices (iphone, ipad and ipod) for 55 participants using survey based test. The results noted few issues with VoiceOver and some interactive elements in Apple apps. Yet, the paper did not examine VoiceOver interactions with mobile web apps.

Given this gap in the domain, we intend to evaluate VoiceOver screen reader accessibility for mobile web apps whether hosted or packaged as a native app.

4   Methodology

Mobile web apps, in their basic form, and when they fully apply web design best practices, are assumed to have a better accessibility when taking screen readers into account. This is due to the fact that mobile web apps are usually a stripped down version that contains the most basic page elements and crucial information without any overly complex content or large tabular information. Furthermore, mobile web apps are more likely to have less navigation elements which improve the usability of the application using screen readers since the user will have less repetitive content to skip.

To conduct the study we built a sample mobile web app adhering to mobile web design best practices. The sample app employs many recent web technologies including HTML5, CSS3, JavaScript and jQuery. The test web app consists of three different pages with various common page elements that are usually problematic. All pages contain a heading section, navigation section, a main content section and a footer (see Figure 1).

Fig. 1. (left) App home page (Right) App form

All these components are coded using their appropriate semantic tag elements provided by HTML5. The main content of the home page is three tabs coded using jQuery. The first tab is selected by default while the other two tabs have initially hidden content. The second page's main content is complex nested lists including Definition, Ordered and Unordered list and an image. The third page contains a form that is built using Forms 2.0 elements including text, email, date, number, radio button and a submit button.

We validated the code of the test web app using W3C's HTML validator and CSS validator which ensured the correctness of the code. Also, the test web app was evaluated using MobileOK (http://validator.w3.org/mobile/), which evaluates the website against W3C MobileOK Basic Tests 1.0. Regrettably, the test web app score could not exceed 54% which is due to MobileOK checker's lack of support of HTML5 and CSS3 syntax in addition to several other errors caused by the static jQuery library.

To evaluate the performance of VoiceOver screen reader, we tested it for both forms of mobile web apps: the browser-based version and the packaged version using PhoneGap. Table 1 shows the characteristics of the testing environment.

Table 1. The characteristics of the tested mobile phone

Mobile device	iPhone 4
OS	iOS 6
Screen Reader	VoiceOver
Default Browser	Safari

The testing procedure was guided by observing three visually impaired users with varying degrees of visual impairment, two were partially-sighted and one was completely blind. The three users were well acquainted with touch screen devices and use them with a screen reader on daily basis. The observation methodology was conducted to understand the exact usage and mentality of the visually impaired users and detect any difficulties or preferences they encounter and/or express when using the test materials. The users were individually requested to access the sample mobile web app using first the web browser and then the native app version. In the session, the moderator observes the participant whose been asked to think out loud while navigating through the app. Also, the moderator would provide help and explanation for participants when needed.

5   Results and Discussions

Based on our observations, we have found some important findings and preferences that are inherent from the touch nature of the tested system. Firstly, the VIP expressed the ease with which they browse the web using the mobile screen reader and the touch interface. They stated that the mobile screen reader is clearer and much more easy to use than the desktop one.

As to their usage preference, which will be useful when designing accessible mobile phone application, we have deducted that visually impaired users prefer sequential access to all pages and application content as opposed to gesturing up or down which gives them a partially spatial random access. It is even preferred over clicking directly on something for our partially sighted testers. They express that sequential access ensures the coverage of all pages or app elements and that they prefer skipping unwanted content than accessing wanted content randomly. They stated that due to the touch screen, they are prone to click on some elements by mistake causing the reader to jump to that element. Thus skipping some important content unknowingly, which arise the need of having a feature that enables changing the position of focused element using the sequential gestures only.   Furthermore, users emphasized on the importance of audio aids given to them by the screen reader that signals certain events including the audio feedback triggered when clicking a link or button, loading a new page, hitting the end of the page, and so on. This is due to the fact that they need to know if they performed a gesture correctly or not. We have also observed that while filling forms, users rely heavily on the 'next' and 'previous' buttons in the keyboard which enable them to navigate through input fields of the form without hiding the keyboard, i.e. they are aware that the keyboard has sprung up, they may be confused when it is hidden again.

Next, we will discuss in further details the results of VoiceOver behaviors while dealing with the mobile app on the browser and as a native app.

5.1   Browser Test

A) Document Structure Awareness (Headings, Lists and Other Elements)
The VoiceOver announces main headings as they are, along with their position among other headings. This results in the success of reflecting the true structure of the page to the user. Another observation in representing the structure is shown when reading the page of nested lists. VoiceOver announces the beginning of a list but not its ending. As to indicate list elements; in the case of Unordered and Ordered list, the screen reader pronounces the word "bullet" at the beginning of each item in the Unordered list or the associated number in the Ordered list. However, when the list is a Definition List (represented in HTML5 using the <dl> element), it was read as the beginning of a list for the first element only; whereas the other elements are announced as if they were simply paragraphs.

VoiceOver does not announce other HTML5 semantic elements such as <article> and <section> to give more information about the page structure. Furthermore, the screen reader does not announce links found in the <nav> element differently than other links, or try to give them special emphasis or provide special access to these links.

B) Audio Aids
When accessing a web page using Safari by entering the page address, VoiceOver screen reader will issue a sound that indicates the page is loading. Then it will issue a small alert when it is done loading the page. Once the page is fully loaded, the screen reader will announce the first element of the page's content. This procedure is repeated whenever a link is clicked and a new page is loaded. Our testers indicated that this specific audio aid triggered when loading and opening a new page is very helpful to let them know they moved into a new view, so they expect a change in content and element positions. They expressed regret that native apps do not support such audio aid.

VoiceOver also provides necessary audio aids at certain places: A special sound is announced when a user moves sequentially toward the end of the page. However this sound will not be announced until the user reaches the end of the navigation bar of Safari which resides at the bottom of the screen where the user cannot navigate further. The screen reader also provides audio aid when scrolling up or down the page with a whistling sound and saying "Page number1 space number2", where number1 representing the current page against the total number of pages (in this case number2). The reader also provides an audio feedback when a link or button has been previously visited.

C) Hidden Content
The screen reader announced tabs clearly stating the currently selected tab, its order and the total number of tabs. It proceeds to read the content of the currently-selected tab without reading the hidden content of other tabs until these tabs are selected by the user.

D) Forms

In the form page, the labels and input areas are announced appropriately. When a text area is reached, the screen reader will announce the need of double tapping the field for editing. When clicked, the keyboard will spring up. A major accessibility drawback in iOS is its lack of audio input method as seen in other mobile operating systems. As to radio buttons and checkboxes, the screen reader announces the button as it is encountered and states whether it is checked or not.

VoiceOver shows support of some features of Forms 2.0, which is apparent in announcing if the input field is free text, and informing the user that it is a required field. However, while the browser has support for Forms 2.0 numerical and date fields, the screen reader itself fails to understand them where it announces them as text fields. This caused great confusion to the users, since the screen reader announces the date field as text field so the VIP expects an alphanumeric keyboard to spring up. However, the date input tool shows that the browser does not announce the type of the adjustable slides (day, month or year).

E) Pictures

When encountering a picture, the reader announces the fact that a picture is there, by simply reading the alternative text followed by the word "Image".

5.2   Native App Test

The native app performance has a similar behavior as browsing the mobile web app using Safari browser. The aim of testing the screen reader against a packaged version of the web app is to ensure the completeness of our test procedure by testing web application in both common forms of their deployment. Furthermore we aimed to detect any differences and unexpected behavior which emerges from changing the underlying run time engine.

VoiceOver immediately announced the app's name then reads first item of the page without going through any context headings and/or browser icons. VoiceOver deals with the native app similarly to the browser version. It announced headings, article sections, links, and so on.

When the ending of the page is reached, a specific audio feedback is given much sooner than the browser version which had to announce the browser controls first.

When navigating through the form, it had the same issues regarding the numeral and date fields.

The only difference found between the two versions of the mobile web app was in the native app; where the screen reader fails to announce the reload of a new page which might confuse the user who is waiting for such an alert.

6   Conclusion and Lessons Learned

In this paper, we presented our experience in evaluating the accessibility of mobile web apps via VoiceOver screen reader and detecting its useful features and shortcomings. Furthermore, this study shows that there are no big differences in the performance between mobile web app accessed via the browser or as native app when using Voice-Over. Thus developers may opt for either option without compromising the accessibility of their apps.

Additionally, during the testing process with the aid of visually impaired testers who use the mobile screen reader daily, we compiled a list of suggested guidelines and recommendations for web developers to maximize the accessibility and usability of their mobile web apps.

- We have found that the Browser based Web app header section and navigation bar are only relevant and important in the first landing page. On subsequent pages it becomes more of a hindrance to the VIP and they skip it most of the time. Later, when the users finish reading the page, they need to travel back to the navigation bar. Hence, placing the Web App name and navigation link at the end of internal pages promotes its usability.
- VIP users who use screen readers to navigate through the web app prefer a gesture (most commonly left and right) to be used to navigate through internal pages of the web app instead of using tabs.
- Screen readers are yet to support some advanced Forms 2.0 elements, while browsers do support them which may create some confusion to users. We recommend expressing explicitly the nature of the text field (i.e. Text, Date, Numbers Only, etc.) in the label of the input element. Furthermore, the browser does not support form validation yet, and upon entering invalid input or forgetting a required field, the browser reloads the page giving focus to the erroneous element without any explanatory error message. So we suggest the inclusion of value validation code with accessible error messages.

These basic guidelines can be further studied to come up with design recommendations for designing accessible mobile web apps for VIP. Furthermore, mobile screen readers show great ability to understand new structural elements provided by HTML5, so we recommend using them in a correct and representational manner.

Finally, although the study led to valuable results, there were some unavoidable limitations. First, the small number of test subjects entailed in this experiment is used for preliminary assessment rather than a full experiment. Second, the study tested VoiceOver screen reader only while excluding TalkBack, because of Android's various OS releases and devices that led to inconsistent behavior of the web app through multiple devices. Lastly, the developed mobile app did not include all HTML 5 elements; it only concentrated on the most common elements used to ensure that each session will not be too long for the participants.

References

[1] What is a Screen Reader? – Humanising Technology Blog,
     http://www.nomensa.com/blog/2005/what-is-a-screen-reader/
     (accessed January 29, 2013)

[2] Make your iOS app accessible with VoiceOver | Feature | .net magazine, http://www.netmagazine.com/features/ make-your-ios-app-accessible-voiceover (accessed February 12, 2013)

[3] The WebKit Open Source Project, http://www.webkit.org/ (accessed January 28, 2013)

[4] Sandhya, S., Devi, K.A.S.: Accessibility evaluation of websites using screen reader. In: 2011 7th International Conference on Next Generation Web Services Practices (NWeSP), pp. 338–341 (2011)

[5] Buzzi, M.C., Buzzi, M., Leporini, B., Mori, G., Penichet, V.M.R.: Accessing Google docs via screen reader. In: Miesenberger, K., Klaus, J., Zagler, W., Karshmer, A. (eds.) ICCHP 2010, Part I. LNCS, vol. 6179, pp. 92–99. Springer, Heidelberg (2010)

[6] Buzzi, M.C., Buzzi, M., Leporini, B.: Accessing e-Learning Systems via Screen Reader: An Example. In: Jacko, J.A. (ed.) HCII 2009, Part IV. LNCS, vol. 5613, pp. 21–30. Springer, Heidelberg (2009)

[7] Buzzi, M.C., Buzzi, M., Leporini, B., Akhter, F.: Usability and Accessibility of eBay by Screen Reader. In: Holzinger, A., Miesenberger, K. (eds.) USAB 2009. LNCS, vol. 5889, pp. 500–510. Springer, Heidelberg (2009)

[8] Chen, Y.-L., Ho, Y.-Y.: The status of using 'Big Eye' Chinese screen reader on 'Wretch' blog in Taiwan. In: Proceedings of the 2007 International Cross-Disciplinary Conference on Web Accessibility (W4A), New York, NY, USA, pp. 134–135 (2007)

[9] Leporini, B., Buzzi, M.C., Buzzi, M.: Interacting with mobile devices via VoiceOver: usability and accessibility issues. In: Proceedings of the 24th Australian Computer-Human Interaction Conference, New York, NY, USA, pp. 339–348 (2012)

Students' Perspectives on Utility of Mobile Applications in Higher Education

Naghmeh Aghaee and Ken Larsson

Department of Computer and System Sciences,
Stockholm University, Stockholm, Sweden
{nam,kenlars}@dsv.su.se

Abstract. Use of Information and Communication Technologies (ICT) in pedagogy and learning in higher education supports the concept of Technology Enhanced Learning (TEL). Mobile devices and applications with educational purposes are part of using online ICT and facilitate autonomous learning in education. Using mobile applications for education has significantly improved in the last few years. However, there is still a gap, in which this concept is still not widely known and frequently experienced by learners. As a part of supporting TEL in higher education and filling this gap, the department of Computer and System Sciences at Stockholm University in Sweden is planning to develop a mobile application for the SciPro system. SciPro is the computer-mediated communication platform to support enhancement of thesis quality and facilitate autonomous learning in higher education, at both Bachelor and Master levels. This study aims to investigate and evaluate learners' perspectives about utility of mobile applications in higher education and specifically to support SciPro functionalities. Almost 95% of the respondents use mobile applications for higher education and believe in the utility of mobile applications for supporting learning in higher education. This is while there are a few respondents (less than 5%), who do not fully share this opinion. More than 70% of the respondents think that a SciPro mobile application will add value to their thesis process. Even though it may not directly affect the speed and quality of the thesis, it will increase mobility, availability, and flexibility of accessing information and resources in SciPro.

Keywords: Technology Enhanced Learning (TEL), Information and Communication Technologies (ICT), Mobile Application, Applications, Learning, Higher Education, Thesis Process.

1 Introduction

Technology Enhanced Learning (TEL) is a concept formed and developed from using Information and Communication Technologies (ICT) in pedagogy and learning. Appropriate use of online ICT for mobile devices and applications facilitates autonomous learning in education. Most of the applications, which are software programs for smart phones, tablets, and other hand-held devices, are designed narrowly for specific

M. Matera and G. Rossi (Eds.): MobiWIS 2013 Workshops, CCIS 183, pp. 44–56, 2013.
© Springer International Publishing Switzerland 2013

purposes. There are several applications with educational purposes, which are developed to facilitate autonomous learning in higher education. However, this number of applications in comparison to the total number of existing applications for mobile devices is still too low. Furthermore, with the intuitive nature of application development for mobile devices, applications are mostly developed toward parent-child anticipations for children rather than educational purposes for learners.

On the challenge of using ICTs to support TEL, a better connection between 'technological' and 'pedagogical' perspectives is required [1]. As a part of supporting TEL, the Department of Computer and System Sciences (DSV) at Stockholm University, in Sweden, has developed a computer-mediated communication (CMC) platform called SciPro [2-8]. SciPro is developed to support the enhancement of thesis quality and to facilitate autonomous learning in higher education. As a complementary tool for improvement of learners' interactions, learner-learner, learner-content, and learner-instructor interactions, as defined by Moore [9], a mobile application will be developed for SciPro to provide further support for learners.

In learning style, there is a big transformation from traditional courses to graduation work for students, from focusing on information processing in courses, students are in the graduation work expected to focus on knowledge creation. This new learning style includes mastering independent thinking, test and redo, defending and in-depth argument for the work conducted [10, 11]. The student who is working on a thesis is in many respect facing the same opportunities and threats as a distance student, with similar barriers from completing the studies [12]. Therefore the experience of successful strategies for distance learning may be successful also in thesis work. Utilizing the successful solutions of on and off campus settings [13] the proposed system support in this work may reduce these barriers for the students.

1.1   Mobile Computing in Educational Context

In order to propose the priority for developing mobile applications to support the thesis process, there is a need to investigate the role of mobile computing in education. A study of the use of mobile learning Kukulska-Hulme [14] lists some 18 uses, from motivating to strengthening ownership of learning, that are particularly suitable for mobile use. From this list we find five that would be of special interest to pursue as candidates for the first version: alerting, rapid response, information gathering on the go, improved accessibility and personal learning management. The study arrives at three keywords for user benefits: portability, connectivity and convenience [14]. When discussing *usability*, it is often focused on a task the user intends to perform. Transformed to the educational context, this would be equivalent to tasks like studying a material, taking notes, writing a report, communicating with teachers and students. In the educational setting the act of learning may not be as easily broken down in tasks, as each of these may consist of several different actions that are highly individual and dependent on the specific context [15].

One of the objectives of the SciPro system is to reduce barriers for students in completing their theses. There is also the assumption that working with your thesis project

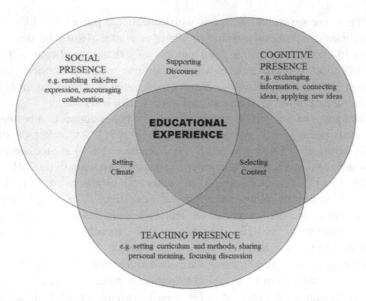

Fig. 1. The Community of Inquiry Model (Source: Garrison, Anderson & Archer [16])

course is in several aspects similar to being a student in a distance course. The Community of Inquiry Model in Figure 1 above proposes some areas that can be utilized to improve the education experiences for students and thus reduce the barriers to study. Anderson takes the approach that social presence is an appropriate way of improving the experience [17]. One of the features mentioned by Anderson is notifications, as this enhances feedback and presence. This is what is specifically taken into consideration in this study to investigate students' perspectives toward *utility* of mobile application notifications. When discussing "*utility*", it refers to serviceability, applicability, appropriateness, and advantage of using mobile applications, to investigate students' perspectives for using applications in higher educations. It may not be obvious what device to use for mobile learning, as most learning activities seems to take place on devices that are not designed with learning in mind [15]. What seems to be important is that the learning content must meet a minimum standard and function adequately [18].

1.2   Aim

The SciPro system is a web-based system to improve the supervision and management of graduation work as well as support the student in completing the thesis work. Some students have expressed a need for a mobile application for some core parts of the system. Our aim with this study is to ascertain if this need is perceived by a larger group of students and, if so, what would be the appropriate functions to include in the first release. The study is intended to gather information on *what* to do rather than *how* to implement the functions, which would require further investigation to get specific data on the preferred design of the specific application. Part of the investigation is to propose one or more suitable models for describing *what* to do and by a survey establish *why* this would be of use for the students. The function of notifications in the form of e-mail is already part of the system; this study is not about finding new notifications, but to provide insight into what notifications are suitable for inclusion in a mobile application.

The significant criterion for devices and applications in education is the values they add to the learning process. Evaluation of learners' perspectives provides valuable information about what matters, which help institutes gain better understanding about requirements and useful services [19, 20]. Hence, this study aims to investigate two main scopes by evaluating students' perspectives: 1) utility of mobile applications in higher education, 2) utility of specific information and notification for SciPro mobile application to provide further support for Bachelor and Master students' thesis work.

Moreover, the objective of this study is connected to different presences of educational experiences, illustrated in Figure 1. As illustrated in the left-hand side's boxes in Figure 2, SciPro provides different functionalities to support the thesis process and

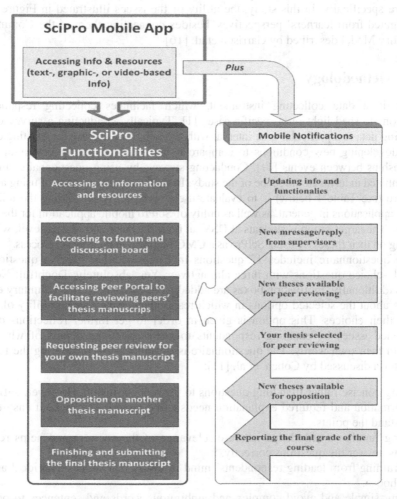

Fig. 2. SciPro functionalities and possible SciPro mobile Application support

enhance the quality of theses. SciPro mobile application would increase mobility, availability and flexibility of accessing existing information and resources in SciPro. Moreover, as illustrated in the right-hand side of the figure, providing notifications in SciPro mobile application would be connected to different SciPro functionalities as additional support for learning and communication.

The question on what environment to implement the mobile application in is important as the first version should reach as many students as possible. Worldwide and in Europe the iOS and Android are the leading environments for mobile applications with approximately 40% market share each. In Sweden there is a different situation where iOS has approximately 65% market share, almost double the android environment according to StatCounter (http://gs.statcounter.com/#mobile_os-SE-monthly-201205-201305-bar). In the targeted age group around 80% own a smart phone in Sweden, after the age of 45 the penetration falls sharply, which is significantly more than the penetration of tablet computers for the target group[21].

More specifically, in this study, the utility of the issues illustrated in Figure 2 are investigated from learners' perspectives, besides connecting them to the Community of Inquiry Model described by Garrison et al. [16].

2   Methodology

Survey is a data collecting instrument, which facilitates collecting respondents' reflections to shed light on a specific case [11]. Typically, conducting a survey entails collecting data at a particular time interval with the aim of describing the existing conditions, developing new conditions to compare to the existing one, or determining the relationships between events [11]. Conducting surveys by using questionnaires may be differentiated in terms of the scope of the study. In this study, the purpose of using a questionnaire (see Table 1 below) is to evaluate users' perspectives regarding the utility of mobile applications in general, as well as utility of SciPro mobile application for the thesis process. The target group is students at DSV, at both Bachelor and Master level, who are working on their theses by using SciPro as a CMC platform in their thesis process.

The questionnaire includes 12 questions in English, either Yes/No questions or multiple-choice questions with three alternatives: Yes, absolutely; Doubtful; No, not at all. Additionally, motivation boxes are added to five questions, for voluntary explanations about the selected options in which respondents have the possibility of motivating their choices. This option is given in order to get further reflections on the questioned issues by enabling respondents to write about the details of what they think, in their own words. The questionnaire is developed by considering the following criteria discussed by Cohen, et al. [11]:

— Using concise rather than long questions to prevent confusion. However, sufficient information and required explanation needs to be provided to make it easy to understand the points.
— Using familiar words helps increase relevance of the answers and helps respondents answer the questions correctly.
— Refraining from leading respondents' mind in a way that suggests an ideal answer to choose.
— Being simple and avoid complex and ambiguous words and sentences to prevent misinterpretations.

The twelve questions (Table 1 below) are developed based on the criteria above, in addition to what Anderson discusses about notifications [15] and what Garrison et al. describe in the Community of Inquiry Model [16]. Furthermore, motivation boxes are complimentary data collection techniques for eliciting detailed information, social objections and further suggestions. This will increase the validity of the study, since there will be reasoning behind the chosen options by the respondents.

Table 1. The questions respondents where asked to respond to

Q nbr	Question	Answer options
1	Do you use any mobile devices (i.e., smart phone, tablet), which support online applications?	Yes/No
2	Do you use one or more application regularly on your mobile device?	Yes/No
3	Have you ever used any application for educational purposes?	Yes/No
	If so, which application?	Open
4	Do you think mobile applications are useful for supporting learning in higher education?	Yes, absolutely/ Doubtful/ No, not at all
	Please motivate your answer (voluntary)	Open
5	Would an online mobile application for SciPro help you to speed up your thesis process?	Yes, absolutely/ Doubtful/ No, not at all
	Please motivate your answer (voluntary)	Open
6	Would an online mobile application motivate you to have more communication with your supervisor, ex., to get notifications from them when they post messages in Forum?	Yes, absolutely/ Doubtful/ No, not at all
	Please motivate your answer (voluntary)	Open
7	Would an online mobile application motivate you to have more peer communications with your fellows, ex., via forum, chat or email functions?	Yes, absolutely/ Doubtful/ No, not at all
	Please motivate your answer (voluntary)	Open
	Would an online mobile application be useful for you to get notice of ...	
8	... when your supervisor post a new message or answers your questions in the forum?	Yes, absolutely/ Doubtful/ No, not at all
9	... when a new thesis manuscript is uploaded and available for peer reviewing in SciPro peer portal?	Yes, absolutely/ Doubtful/ No, not at all
10	... when your thesis manuscripts has been selected by another student to be peer reviewed?	Yes, absolutely/ Doubtful/ No, not at all
11	... when there is a new thesis manuscript uploaded and available for opposition?	Yes, absolutely/ Doubtful/ No, not at all
12	... when there is an update about SciPro resources or a new functionality available for SciPro?	Yes, absolutely/ Doubtful/ No, not at all

3   Findings

Survey Procedure and Background Data. The questionnaire is sent to the DSV students with active thesis projects during the time interval of January 1, 2012 and April 1, 2013. The questionnaire was open for receiving answers between April 12 and 19, 2013. There might always be additional info by more respondents. Nevertheless, the result of the survey was quite similar with no radical changes after a certain number of responses. Even the named applications used by the users were mainly repeated. The age interval of the respondents is between 21 and 50, with 58% male and 42% female. Based on question one and two, 95% of respondents use mobile devices (i.e., smart phone, tablet), which support online applications, and they use one or more applications regularly on their mobile devices. Based on question three and four, more than half of the respondents have used at least one application for educational purposes. Below, there is a list of applications that respondents report that they have used for educational purposes. Some of these applications have been mentioned by more than 20 respondents.

- Various internet browser applications, such as Safari.
- Various language support applications, such as dictionaries, word translators, languages learning applications, Kindle language, and Babbel.
- Google applications, such as Google translate, Google drive, Google droid (Scholar Droid), YouTube for watching lectures.
- Specific DSV applications, such as First Class and webmail.
- Applications for information/file saving/transferring, such as various E-mail client services, Dropbox, Notes/memo, Voice memo, ToDo, Evernote, Photos as a note taking tool in the lectures and seminars, calendar for daily scheduling and academic appointments.
- Additional applications, such as Wikipedia, GRE Preparation, 1Password, GoodReader, Adobe Acrobat Reader (PDF reader), video player (for DSV or other recorded lectures), iTunes U (for university lectures).

Mobile Application Utility (based on question five to twelve): more than 80% of respondents think that mobile applications are useful for supporting learning in higher education. Many respondents believe that the SciPro application would be very useful. This is while only one third of them think that SciPro mobile application would help speed up the thesis process, or support student-supervisor or peer-peer communication. The following issues are what they mentioned as significant benefits of using mobile applications, in general, as well as specifically for SciPro in the thesis process. As mentioned by a respondent, *"a major advantage of mobile applications is its mobility and the possibility to access data at any time and any place"*. In the thesis process in higher education, this could mean that students can use mobile applications to check their studies' status and information on the way from or to campus. Mobile devices are often carried by users, which makes it easier for them to engage in learning everywhere they go. The applications would provide great opportunities by providing access to schedules, course information, library indices, etc.

Using applications for educational purposes supports learners to have universal access to the existing information, save time or using their time efficiently, collaborate with their fellows, and enhance communications. Mobile devices and applications can be useful for higher education to the same degree as for basic education. Its flexibility makes the process of learning and updating faster for the learners. The mobile applications help getting information faster besides having all data with you all the time and being accessible any time as long as the device is with you, which is the case with mobile phones. These factors are useful to facilitate an increased educational experience as they can be used to increase the various forms of presence as discussed by Garrison et al [16] in the Community of Inquiry Model for education, see Figure 1. As mentioned by many respondents, some applications are excellent to facilitate reviewing, updating, modifying, responding and communicating in critical situations, when immediate intervention is needed.

Like any other useful mobile applications, SciPro application would also support accessing important school information, effectively replacing PCs. This is while another learner mentions "*Possibly useful as a supplement, but not as a substitute*". Most likely as any other ICT in TEL, this application would also have significant features for enhancing the learning process. "*It provides the easiness to access Scipro, anytime, even when travelling and you can access the forum and other related information while you are mobile*". The mobility and interaction when using mobile devices are different than desktop computers. As long as the mobile device is on, it enables the user to have access to the data and get any updates on time.

SciPro mobile application may speed up the communication, but would not directly affect the actual work process speed. It makes getting updates easier and faster, especially for finding a thesis for opposition or active participation, since it is sometimes so hard to find one and students need to log in to SciPro every day and keep checking. Students can read supervisors' feedback through the SciPro mobile application, but not so much more to enhance communications. Communication might be easier and faster when it comes to student-supervisor or peer discussions, but not for transferring files. More than half of the respondents agree that the SciPro application would be useful for getting different kinds of notifications. The percentages of respondents for each issue vary, as shown in the Table 1.

Table 2. Mobile application types of notifications

Would an online mobile application be useful for you to get notice of …	% of respondents	Type of presence in fig 1
… when your supervisor post a new message or answers your questions in the forum?	79%	Teaching presence
… when your thesis manuscripts has been selected by another student to be peer reviewed?	70%	Social presence
… when there is a new thesis manuscript uploaded and available for opposition?	63%	Cognitive presence
… when a new thesis manuscript is uploaded and available for peer reviewing in SciPro peer portal?	62%	Social presence
… when there is an update about SciPro resources or a new functionality available for SciPro?	57%	Teaching presence

This is while there are two other much smaller groups of respondents, who do not share the same opinion as the ones in the first group. The learners in the second group are doubtful about the necessity and usability of the online applications in higher education. They think that there might not be a need for working on school tasks and thesis everywhere, such as in the subway. *"People should focus more on real work on real computers. Smart phones are usually more of a distraction that blurs reality/work/fun/rest"*. Students who write their thesis have mainly access to desktop computers; so there would not be much difference by having a mobile application for SciPro. They also mentioned that almost all students, at least at DSV, use computers for working on their theses; hence a mobile application would not be necessary. This group is quite skeptical about the usability and utility of mobile applications for learning and educational purposes. In addition, the last group encompasses very few respondents (5%), who have not yet used mobile applications, so they are not sure how it works and whether online mobile applications would be supporting education in general or thesis process specifically.

4   Discussion

The respondents in the first group see a great potential for education, based on three most significant advantages of mobile applications for higher education purposes, which are: accessibility, availability and flexibility. They believe using applications makes availability of and accessibility to information 24/7, in an easier and more efficient way. Mobile applications could be very useful for education as long as the focus is put both on educational aspects and the application's functionalities for supporting users' needs. The value that the mobile applications would add to the users is a significant issue that is mentioned by several learners.

Having a concrete and focused application for supporting SciPro functionalities, in order to reduce the need of using several additional applications would be a valuable support for learners. SciPro application could be useful for accessing info, getting notifications, getting the final thesis grade, which are so much of interest for learners. However, part of the respondents were doubtful about the value SciPro application may add to speed up the process or support learner-supervisor or peers-peer communication directly. As discussed by Anderson, notifications are important and useful to enhance feedback and presence. As shown in Table 1, more than 50% of the respondents think that notifications would be useful for the SciPro application. The respondents believe in the use of notifications for communication purposes rather than getting updated about available information and resources. Almost 80% of the respondents are positive about using SciPro application for getting notifications to speed up the communications with their supervisors or peers through students' forum and discussion boards. However, they mainly believe that this should not involve attached documents or more complicated tasks through mobile applications.

Having all thesis related info and getting direct notification from SciPro application, rather than through email, would definitely be useful and help save time. Sometimes, students have to wait for a while to find a peer reviewer or opponent for their thesis manuscripts. As shown in Table 1, more than two-thirds of the students agree that the SciPro mobile application would be useful to make this process faster and easier. Moreover, in order to find a specific notification or forum message, learners can save time to use the mobile application instead of searching through all email's inbox and other folders. Many of the learners believe that SciPro might provide further support for communications and make the process more convenient, but probably not directly influence the quality of the thesis or help speed up the process of writing the thesis.

However, the second and third groups of learners, which are much smaller groups (in total less than 20% of the respondents), do not share these opinions. The respondents in the second group do not see the necessity of working on school tasks and specifically the thesis everywhere. And the third group is still a bit away from using TEL through ICT and mobile technologies, both in their life and education. Hence, they have no idea whether it might support education or not.

Useful Functions for SciPro Mobile Application. Based on more than 70% of respondents, information and notifications would be useful to have access everywhere through the SciPro mobile application. Receiving notifications would be helpful if it is regarding: 1) SciPro info/resources update, 2) when here is a new thesis manuscript for peer review or opposition, 3) a new reviewer is assigned to students' own thesis, and 4) when students get posts from supervisors or fellow students on the forum, chat, or discussion board. Reminders could be another useful function in order to prevent missing deadlines, seminars or supervision appointments. It would also be useful to access available information resources, like design science material, thesis process, templates, available videos etc. Moreover, besides the forum and discussion boards, a chat client or a way to facilitate synchronous communication with supervisors or peers when they are online may be of big use to the learners. Accessing the checklists and reading the instructions, guidelines, comments or even watching online related videos through the application would be convenient and helpful. Availability to the tips, videos, and forums, like a mini social networking site for students discussing and motivating each other with similar topics may be useful.

The functionalities of the application need to be clear and user friendly. Possibility of choosing type of notifications the users would like to receive is an important issue for designing the application. It may be useful for getting the study results, in which students are interested in knowing when it comes. What some learners mentioned is that supervisors probably also need to have a similar application, so that they can access information, as well as get reminders and notifications when students need them or want to ask for help.

Potential Problems. The screens of mobile devices are too small so that users have to scroll up and down to read something thoroughly, which may lead to missing important data. The mobile device is normally moving so much for instance on the train or subway. Therefore, it may influence negatively on the concentration, besides having some negative effects on body and eyes. Moreover, the application may support making little mental to-do-lists after looking over the thesis progress in SciPro, but file compatibility may be an issue. To send ".docx" files and open it in iOS application might cause much trouble and cause some file damages and loss of data. Moreover, temporary application, such as an application only for supporting the thesis work, which will be used for one semester, may not attract many users. It may not be worth learning how to work with it, installing it and using it for a short while.

5   Conclusion

Mobile applications are mostly welcome and appreciated for the computer generation learners. As mentioned in theory, three keywords for user benefits are portability, connectivity and convenience. These are almost the same as what was mentioned by most of the respondents in this study to use mobile applications in higher education: accessibility and availability, flexibility, and mobility in time and geographical places. In this study, respondents belong to three groups: very positive towards the usability and utility of mobile applications in general as well as specifically for SciPro (approximately 80%); doubtful about the usability and utility of applications in education, especially for SciPro (approximately 15%); and the last group encompasses respondents (approximately 5%), who have not used mobile applications and have no idea whether it would be beneficial for education and for SciPro.

According to the theory and empirical data of this study, alerting (notifications), rapid response (support communication), information gathering on the go (availability of accessing info and getting updated info 24/7), and improved accessibility and personal learning management (flexibility and availability of info and notifications whenever needed and wished) are five values that most of the learners think mobile applications, including the SciPro applications, would add to higher education. These five important issues are mentioned as added values by mobile applications in education by more than 70% of the respondents. Moreover, mobile applications in education, such as the SciPro application, would facilitate learners' mobility and accessibility to info and resources, as well as provide support for communications in different presences of educational experiences, mainly through the use of notifications.

In conclusion, based on learners' perspectives, most learners believe in the utility of mobile application in higher education, in which they make it faster, easier and more flexible. According to the result of the study, the SciPro app, would also sufficiently add the specified values (illustrated in Figure 2) as additional support to the SciPro system, in Bachelor's and Master's thesis process. However, this may not directly affect the thesis quality and increase the speed of the thesis writing process, but it supports learners' interactions in all three phases of learner-learner, learner-content, and learner-instructor interactions. We also recommend that the work on developing notifications for the first version focuses on the top five list in Table 1, as these are the most favored by students as useful in the thesis process. These five types also enhance all types of presence in the Community of Inquiry Model, described in Figure 1.

References

1. Richards, C.: Towards an integrated framework for designing effective ICT supported learning environments: The challenge to better link technology and pedagogy. Technology, Pedagogy and Education 15(2), 239–255 (2006)
2. Hallberg, D., et al.: SciPro from a mobile perspective: Technology enhanced supervision of thesis work in emerging regions. In: Aitec East Africa ICT summit at Oshwal Centre, Nairobi, Kenya (2011)
3. Aghaee, N., Hansson, H.: Peer Portal: Quality enhancement in thesis writing using self-managed peer review on a mass scale. The International Review of Research in Open and Distance Learning 14(1), 186–203 (2013)
4. Aghaee, N.M., Larsson, U., Hansson, H.: Improving the Thesis Process. In: The 35th Information Systems Research Seminar in Scandinavia, IRIS 2012 (2012)
5. Hansson, H.: 4-excellence: IT system for theses. Going Global: Internationalising higher education. In: British Council Conference, London (2012)
6. Hansson, H., Moberg, J.: Quality processes in technology enhanced thesis work. In: 24th ICDE World Conference on Open and Distance Learning, Bali, Indonesia (2011)
7. Hansson, H., et al.: SCI-PRO: Improving Universities Core Activity with ICT Supporting the Scientific Thesis Writing Process. In: Sixth EDEN Research Workshop, Budapest (2010)
8. Hansson, H., Larsson, K., Wettergren, G.: Open and flexible ICT - support for student thesis production - design concept for the future. In: Gaskell, A., Mills, R., Tait, A. (eds.) The Cambridge International Conference on Open and Distance Learning, pp. 197–204. The Open University, Cambridge (2009)
9. Moore, M.G.: Editorial: Three types of interaction. American Journal of Distance Education 3(2) (1989)
10. Creswell, J.W.: Research design: Qualitative, quantitative, and mixed methods approaches. Sage Publications, Inc. (2009)
11. Cohen, L., et al.: Research methods in education. Psychology Press (2007)
12. Muilenburg, L.Y., Berge, Z.L.: Student barriers to online learning: A factor analytic study. Distance Education 26(1), 29–48 (2005)
13. Cho, S.K., Berge, Z.L.: Overcoming barriers to distance training and education. USDLA Journal 16(1), 16–34 (2002)
14. Kukulska-Hulme, A.: Current uses of wireless and mobile learning. JISC-funded Landscape Study Report 15, 2006 (2005)
15. Kukulska-Hulme, A.: Mobile usability in educational contexts: what have we learnt? The International Review of Research in Open and Distance Learning 8(2) (2007)
16. Garrison, D.R., Anderson, T., Archer, W.: Critical inquiry in a text-based environment: Computer conferencing in higher education. The Internet and Higher Education 2(2), 87–105 (1999)
17. Anderson, T.: Distance learning–Social software's killer ap? In: The Open and Distance Learning Association of Australia Conference, Breaking Down Boundaries, Adelaide (2005)
18. Rekkedal, T., Dye, A.: Mobile Distance Learning with PDAs: Development and testing of pedagogical and system solutions supporting mobile distance learners. The International Review of Research in Open and Distance Learning 8(2) (2007)

19. Kuo, Y.-C., et al.: A Predictive Study of Student Satisfaction in Online Education Programs. The International Review of Research in Open and Distance Learning 14(1), 16–39 (2013)
20. Reinhart, J., Schneider, P.: Student satisfaction, self-efficacy, and the perception of the two-way audio/video distance learning environment. A preliminary examination. The Quarterly Review of Distance Education 4(4), 357–365 (2001)
21. Findahl, O.: Swedes and the Internet 2012. The Internet Infrastructure Foundation, Stockholm (2012)

Deferred Retrieval of IoT Information Using QLM Messaging Interface

Sylvain Kubler*, Manik Madhikermi, and Kary Främling

Aalto University, School of Science, Espoo, Finland
P.O. Box 15400, FI-00076 Aalto, Finland
sylvain.kubler@aalto.fi

Abstract. Internet of Things (IoT) is intended to provide a network where information flows could easily be retrieved and set up between any kinds of products, devices, users, *etc.* Quantum Lifecycle Management messaging interface (QLM-MI) has been designed accordingly, providing generic and standardized application-level interfaces. One cornerstone property of QLM-MI provides the opportunity to subscribe IoT information from any "Thing" so as to retrieve it in a deferred way. Subscriptions can be performed to receive a "continuous" data flow or can be based on "client-initiated" communications. All these features are described in this paper, and then a technical proof-of-concept is provided based on a scenario in the framework of smart home.

Keywords: Internet of things, Quantum Lifecycle Management, Intelligent product, Smart house.

1 Introduction

IoT refers to a world where physical objects and beings, as well as virtual data and environments, all interact with each other in the same space and time [1]. Connections are not just people to people or people to computers, but people to things and most strikingly, things to things. IoT is becoming increasingly popular in a wide range of sectors (manufacturing, transportation, smart home, health-care, and so on) [2,3]. In the context of closed-loop product lifecycle management [4], IoT is used as a generic information system for accessing and synchronizing any kind of product-related information over the Internet. In this context, products can have varying degrees of "intelligence", which can range from simple barcodes or RFID tags to vehicles and other products that have advanced sensing, actuating, memory and communication capabilities [5,6].

Quantum Lifecycle Management messaging interface (QLM-MI) was created[1] to enable any kind of intelligent product to exchange IoT information in ad hoc, loosely coupled ways. The lifecycle concept of QLM-MI signifies that information exchange standards have to be able to provide interoperability between

---

* Corresponding author.
[1] http://www.opengroup.org/getinvolved/workgroups/qlm

M. Matera and G. Rossi (Eds.): MobiWIS 2013 Workshops, CCIS 183, pp. 57–65, 2013.

products and with all other information systems that consume or provide relevant information in the product lifecycle. QLM-MI specifications respond to requirements of several real-life industrial applications of the PROMISE (Product Lifecycle Management and Information Tracking Using Smart Embedded Systems: www.promise.no) EU FP6 project [4], the main ones are:

- possible to implement for any kind of information systems, including embedded and mobile systems,
- not restricted to one communication protocol only, it must be possible to send messages using protocols such as plain HTTP, SOAP, SMTP,
- support for "synchronous" messaging as immediate read/write operations, including "client-poll" subscriptions,
- handling mobility and intermittent network connectivity, i.e. support for asynchronous messaging capabilities, message consistence, time-to-live functionality,
- historical queries, i.e. retrieving values between two points in time.

This paper provides an overview of the QLM-MI standards proposal that fulfill these requirements. QLM-MI combines the main features of asynchronous, enterprise messaging protocols with those of instant messaging protocols in a way that allows for peer-to-peer type communication. Section 2 first gives insight into the QLM-MI properties. Among them, a fundamental one enables a *Thing A*[2] to subscribe any information from another *Thing B*. The subscription can be performed to receive a "continuous" data flow from *Thing B*, but also provides the opportunity to perform a "client-initiated" communication (most of the solutions do not provide this second opportunity). Section 3 presents these two types of subscription. The main contribution of this paper is to provide a technical proof-of-concept of the subscription property, which is provided by the case study in section 4 (defined in the framework of smart home).

2   QLM Messaging Interface

In practice, no suitable standards were found to fulfill the different requirements mentioned in section 1. In addition to EPC-related standards, such as STEP, MIMOSA, PLCS and DPWS were considered [7]. In practice there seemed to be "too many" standards already but they all tended to be too domain-, technology- or lifecycle phase-specific [8]. Accordingly, PROMISE created two main specifications that fulfilled the necessary requirements: the PROMISE Messaging Interface (PMI) and the PROMISE System Object Model (SOM). At the end of the PROMISE project, the work on these standards proposals was moved to the QLM workgroup of The Open Group (http://www.opengroup.org/qlm/). This paper presents the standard proposal derived from PMI, i.e. QML-MI.

In the QLM-MI world, communication between the participants, e.g. products and backend systems, is done by passing messages between nodes using interfaces

---

[2] A "Thing" is also referred to as a "QLM node" in this paper.

Fig. 1. QLM "Cloud"

defined in QLM-MI. The QLM-MI "cloud" in Fig. 1 is intentionally drawn in the same way as for the Internet cloud. Where the Internet uses the HTTP protocol for transmitting HTML-coded information mainly intended for human users, QLM-MI is used for transmitting lifecycle-related information mainly intended for automated processing by information systems[3]. In the same way as HTTP can be used for transporting payloads also in other formats than HTML, QLM-MI can be used for transporting payloads in nearly any format. XML might currently be the most common text-based payload format but others such as JSON, CSV can be used. In total, 7 major properties of QLM-MI can be listed:

1. *QLM-MI messages are **self-contained***: messages can be transported using most "lower-level" protocols such as HTTP, SOAP, FTP or similar protocols. It can also be transported using files on USB sticks or other memory devices. This non-dependency on specific communication protocols makes QLM-MI different from many other potential IoT messaging standards,
2. *three possible operations*:
   - **QLM-MI write:** used for sending information updates to QLM nodes. This involves a QLM-MI response to inform the message originator about the success or failure of the operation,
   - **QLM-MI read**: used for
     - immediate retrieval of information. This involves a QLM-MI response from the targeted QLM node to return the requested information,
     - placing subscriptions for deferred retrieval of information from a QLM node. This is done with a QLM-MI read query if the interval parameter has been set. If:
       * a **callback address** is provided, then the data is sent using a QLM-MI response at the requested interval,
       * **no callback address** is provided, then the data can be retrieved (polled) by issuing a new QLM-MI read query with the ID of the subscription,

---

[3] QLM-MI resides in the Application layer of the Open Systems Interconnection (OSI) model.

- **QLM-MI cancel:** used to cancel subscriptions before they expire. This involves a QLM-MI response to inform the message originator about the success or failure of the operation.

3. *all queries and responses can specify a **time-to-live***: if the message has not been delivered to the "next" node before time-to-live expires, then the message should be removed and an error message returned to the message originator, if possible,

4. *allowing different **payload** formats*: a QLM-MI message (whether query or response) can transport actual information using any text-based format that can be embedded into an XML message. It is even possible to use different payload formats in different return elements of a QLM-MI response,

5. *allowing **synchronous** ("real-time") communication between nodes*: any QLM-MI response can include a new query, which is useful for instance in control applications. It also provides a possibility to perform "client-initiated" communication with nodes that are located behind a firewall,

6. ***publication and discovery** of data sources, services and meta-data*: publication of new data sources, services and meta-data can be done with QLM-MI write operation. "RESTful" URL-based queries allow the discovery of them, including discovery by search engines,

7. *all queries can specify a list of **target QLM nodes***: the receiving node(s) are then responsible of re-routing the query to the target QLM nodes, or sending back an error message to the requesting QLM node in case of failure.

QLM-MI can be applied to virtually any kind of information, i.e. not only physical products but also to document repositories, *etc.*. Querying for available design documents (e.g. CAD documents); subscribing to the addition/deletion/-modification of documents; subscribing to particular change events in design documents is conceptually similar to queries and subscriptions for physical products. As mentioned, the "subscription" property is a cornerstone of QLM-MI. The conceptual framework used here is the Observer Design Pattern presented by [9], which signifies that a QLM node can add itself as an observer of events that occur at another QLM node. In this sense, QLM-MI differs from other messaging models such as JMS, which is based on the Publish-Subscribe model. For many applications, the Observer and the Publish-Subscribe models can be used in quite similar ways. However, the Publish-Subscribe model usually assumes the usage of a "high-availability server", which the Observer pattern does not [10]. For this reason, the Observer model is more suitable for IoT applications where products might communicate with each other directly.

In this paper, a particular focus is given to the property 2, and especially on the two options for placing subscriptions for deferred retrieval of IoT information (i.e. with and without callback).

3 Deferred Retrieval of Information Using "Subscriptions"

In IoT, new objects frequently join and start communicating and existing ones disappear. Currently, there are millions of sensors deployed around the world

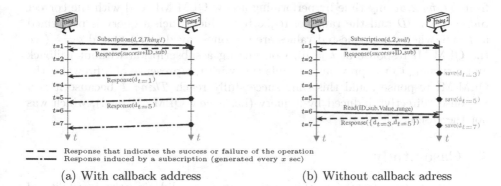

- - - Response that indicates the success or failure of the operation
—·— Response induced by a subscription (generated every x sec)

(a) With callback address   (b) Without callback adress

Fig. 2. Deferred retrieval of information: callback *vs.* no callback

and it is predicted that there will be $50 - 100$ billion devices connected to the Internet by 2020 [11]. Similarly to the number of objects, the number of communications will also increase significantly, thus requiring new types of IoT interactions. QLM-MI aims - in the long term - at covering the vast majority of these interactions and, in this effect, new ones are introduced with QLM-MI through the concept of "subscription".

Fig. 2(a) and 2(b) respectively detail the two types of subscriptions considering two QLM nodes: *Thing 1* and *Thing 2*. In Fig. 2(a), *Thing 1* subscribes a data d on *Thing 2* at $t = 1$, providing its address as callback with an interval of 2 units of time[4]. A response is first sent by *Thing 2* to *Thing 1* both to confirm the correct reception of its QLM-MI read and to provide it with the ID of the subscription (see the response at $t = 1$). Then, every 2 units of time, *Thing 2* sends to *Thing 1* the current data d value (again through a QLM response as depicted at $t = 3, 5, 7, \ldots$). A distinction is made between a "response that indicates the success or failure of the operation" and a "response induced by the subscription (i.e. automatically generated every x units of time)". This distinction is of particular importance in presence of a firewall. Let us consider a firewall that does not permit *Thing 2* to reach *Thing 1* but does the opposite; the QLM-MI response at $t = 1$ could successfully reach *Thing 1* because the firewall always authorizes a response subsequent to a query. However, the QLM-MI responses sent by *Thing 2* at $t = 3, 5, 7, \ldots$ will be stopped by the firewall because they are not "directly" induced by a query, but automatically generated after x units of time.

In Fig. 2(b), *Thing 1* subscribes a data d on *Thing 2* at $t = 1$, also with an interval of 2 units of time, but this time without providing its address as callback (see the value "*null*" in the Subscription performed at $t = 1$). Accordingly, *Thing 2* saves the current data d value every 2 units of time (see *save($d_{t=3}$)*, *save($d_{t=5}$)*, etc.). *Thing 1* may therefore request one or several historical values

---

[4] The corresponding function in Fig. 2(a) is noted "Subscription(d,x,add)"; d the data to subscribe, x the interval value (in units of time), **add** the callback address.

from *Thing 2* at any time by performing a new QLM-MI read with the correct *Subscription_ID* and the range of requested values. Such a query is performed at $t = 6$, where the requested values are the ones saved at $t = 3$ and $t = 5$ (see the QLM-MI response at $t = 6$). Considering a subscription without callback and returning to the previous example (i.e. with the presence of a firewall), the QLM-MI response could this time successfully reach *Thing 1* because it is a response "directly" induced by a query (i.e. a new QLM-MI read), which was not the case in Fig. 2(a).

4   Case Study

The case study presented in this section aims at validating the feasibility of placing subscriptions between different "Things". Two "Things" are considered in this scenario as illustrated in Fig. 3:

1. *Thing 1*: a node located in a house that monitors the indoor temperature. In our scenario, this node is a *Raspberry PI* connected to a temperature sensor,
2. *Thing 2*: a node that displays the indoor temperature evolution over a time period. This node may be a laptop, a smartphone and could be located anywhere; it is only necessary to have a continuous access to the Internet.

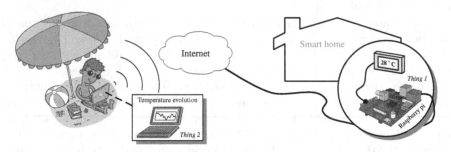

Fig. 3. Illustration of the applicative scenario

In this scenario, the house owner wants to continuously receive the indoor temperature during his/her trip. For this to happen, the house owner (i.e. *Thing 2*) sends a QLM-MI read query for subscribing the temperature data on *Thing 1*. This query is detailed in Fig. 4. The payload format defined in QLM-MI, named "QLM_mf.xsd" in line 4, has been presented in [8]. To briefly summarize it, it is defined as a simple ontology, specified using XML Schema, which is generic enough for representing "any" object and information that is needed for information exchange in the IoT. It is structured as a hierarchy with an "Objects" element as its top element (*cf.* line 4), which can contain any number of "Object" sub-elements (*cf.* line 5). The most important attribute of an Object is "class", which specifies what kind of object it is[5] (line 5 indicates it is "Thing1_Node").

---

[5] An optional attribute called "udef" may be used for specifying the object class using the *Universal Data Element Framework* (UDEF; www.udef.com) taxonomy.

```
1   <qlmEnvelope xmlns="QLM_mi.xsd" version="1.0" ttl="3600">
2     <read msgformat="QLM_mf.xsd" interval="1800" callback="http:
      //207.46.130.1">
3       <msg xmlns:xs="http://www.w3.org/2001/XMLSchema" xmlns:xsi="
          http://www.w3.org/2001/XMLSchema-instance" xsi:type="
          xs:string">
4         <Objects xmlns="QLM_mf.xsd">
5           <Object class="Thing1_Node">
6             <id>Temp_value</id>
7             <InfoItem class="Temperature"></InfoItem>
8             <id>Time_value</id>
9             <InfoItem class="Time"></InfoItem>
10          </Object>
11        </Objects>
12      </msg>
13    </read>
14  </qlmEnvelope>
```

Fig. 4. QLM-MI read (subscription with callback) sent by *Thing 2* to *Thing 1*

```
1   <qlmEnvelope xmlns="QLM_mi.xsd" version="1.0" ttl="3600">
2     <response>
3       <result>
4         <return returnCode="200" /></result>
5         <requestId>REQ654534</requestId>
6         <msg xmlns:xs="http://www.w3.org/2001/XMLSchema" xmlns:xsi="
            http://www.w3.org/2001/XMLSchema-instance" xsi:type="
            xs:string">
7           <Objects>
8             <Object class="Thing1_Node">
9               <id>Temp\_value</id>
10              <InfoItem class="Temperature">
11                <value>27</value>
12              </InfoItem>
13              <InfoItem class="Time">
14                <value>14:00:04</value>
15              </InfoItem>
16            </Object>
17          </Objects>
18        </msg>
19      </result>
20    </response>
21  </qlmEnvelope>
```

Fig. 5. QLM-MI response induced by the subscription (generated every 1800 sec)

"Object" elements can have any number of properties, referred to as InfoItem (line 7 and 9 respectively indicate that this message deals with a property named "Temperature" and another named "Time"). Line 2 indicates that this message is a QLM-MI read query, where the interval parameter is set to "1800" (i.e. 30 min) with a callback address of http://207.46.130.1, meaning that *Thing 1* has to send the indoor temperature at this address every 30 min. Accordingly, this information is sent via QLM-MI responses every 30 min, one of which is detailed in Fig. 5. This response indicates in line 5 that the subscription ID is RED654534 and that, at this specific moment (2 p.m. as indicated line 14), the indoor temperature is of 27 ° C. This scenario was tested throughout a whole day and a generic software application has been designed to allow users to display such information (or similar) on their web browser (e.g. on their mobile devices).

Despite its simplicity, this scenario validates the feasibility of placing subscription for receiving a "continuous" data flow from a distant QLM node. More complex scenarios and applications could further be imagined, e.g. to update CAD documents/simulations in manufacturing applications. This scenario did not present a validation for "client-initiated" communications, but QLM-MI messages used for such communications are similar to those presented in this case study.

5   Conclusion

This paper provides an overview of the QLM Messaging Interface (QLM-MI) standards proposal, which combines the main features of asynchronous, enterprise messaging protocols with those of instant messaging protocols. The main focus of the paper is on a fundamental property that provides the possibility to subscribe (with or without callback) IoT information from a "Things" so as to retrieve it in a deferred way. Subscriptions with callback are particularly useful in applications where it is necessary to receive a "continuous" data flow (e.g. for continuous monitoring, diagnostics, etc.), while subscriptions without callback are particularly useful in cases where "Things" are located behind a firewall.

A technical proof-of-concept of this property is provided by the case study in Section 4. The case study has been specified in an overly simple way because the main purpose here is to provide a validation of such a functionality. However, such a property is essential in most real-life IoT applications, especially due to the expansion of the IoT that requires new types of interactions between "Things". The possibility of placing subscription over a long or a short period of time offers a clear advantage compared to the current state-of-the-art.

References

1. Sundmaeker, H., Guillemin, P., Friess, P., Woelfflé, S.: Vision and challenges for realising the Internet of Things. Cluster of European Research Projects on the Internet of Things, European Commision (2010)
2. Atzori, L., Iera, A., Morabito, G.: The internet of things: A survey. Computer Networks 54(15), 2787–2805 (2010)
3. Barnaghi, P., Wang, W., Henson, C., Taylor, K.: Semantics for the Internet of Things: early progress and back to the future. International Journal on Semantic Web and Information Systems 8(1), 1–21 (2012)
4. Kiritsis, D.: Closed-loop PLM for intelligent products in the era of the internet of things. Computer-Aided Design 43(5), 479–501 (2011)
5. Meyer, G., Främling, K., Holmström, J.: Intelligent products: A survey. Computers in Industry 60(3), 137–148 (2009)
6. McFarlane, D., Giannikas, V., Wong, A.C., Harrison, M.: Product intelligence in industrial control: Theory and practice. Annual Reviews in Control (2013)

7. Villa, M., Rotondi, D., Comolli, M., Seccia, C., Huth, H. P., Kloukinas, C., Trsek, H., Claessens, J.: WP 1 – Plug&Work IoT Requirement assessment and architecture. IoT@ Work (2010)
8. Främling, K., Maharjan, M.: Standardized communication between intelligent products for the IoT. In: 11th IFAC Workshop on Intelligent Manufacturing Systems, São Paulo, Brazil (2013)
9. Gamma, E., Helm, R., Johnson, R., Vlissides, J.: Design patterns: elements of reusable object-oriented software. Addison Wesley Publishing Company, Reading (1995)
10. Eugster, P.T., Felber, P.A., Guerraoui, R., Kermarrec, A.M.: The many faces of publish/subscribe. ACM Computing Surveys 35(2), 114–131 (2003)
11. Perera, C., Zaslavsky, A., Christen, P., Georgakopoulos, D.: Context aware computing for the internet of things: A survey. IEEE Communications Surveys & Tutorials (2013)

A Systematical Scheme of Composite Analysis on Big Sensor-Data of Engineering Inspection

Min-Hwan Ok and Hyun-seung Jung

Korea Railroad Research Institute, Woram, Uiwang, Gyeonggi, Korea
mhok@krri.re.kr

Abstract. Dependencies, associations, correlations, and co-variances found out during big data analysis could unveil the basis of phenomena hard to understand. Recent paradigm of big data analysis has proven its potentiality with big data arose from social activities. Such big data could be generated in some engineering areas, since many kinds of sensors are equipped for researches in engineering. This work presents a scheme of an analysis against big sensor-data in a case of data measured on the railroad. The scheme is composed of procedurees for composite analysis comprised of engineering analyses and big data analysis. A role-based system diagram digests this data-intensive computing of the composite analysis.

Keywords: Big Sensor-Data, Composite Analysis, Data-Intensive Computing, Cloud Computing, Measured Data on the Railroad.

1 Overview

Advancement of instruments raises levels of data volumes in the scientific and engineering fields as higher resolution or rates found more precise or accurate analyses. Consolidated computing resources such as Cloud are also concentrating at processing the data volume larger than ever. Distributed computing resources are managed in the way efficiently allotting resources participating in the same computation considering how they are consolidated into one Cloud.

Sensor data collected by engineering inspection amounts in *Terabytes*, and the data types are mostly in one of three types: (sound) signal, (picture) image or video. In the case the data volume of terabytes is constituted with the data types in signal and image, generated by dozens of sensors, those data are heavy to be processed by an ordinary computing system, such as a single server system. Further if those data are collected against one physical entity for investigation into partitions of the entity, associations and correlations among the data could be revealed. This work schematizes a composite analysis on sensor data measured on the railroad, and stored in the Cloud.

Composite analysis comprises traditional engineering analyses with respective techniques and big data analysis. In the former engineering analyses, a research engineer analyzes the sensor data of a respective partition of the entity, the railroad in this

M. Matera and G. Rossi (Eds.): MobiWIS 2013 Workshops, CCIS 183, pp. 66–71, 2013.

work. The analysis result is input as a context about the partition and some domain parameters are derived from the context. The latter big data analysis involves these parameters, and the context enlarges domain knowledge in the Cloud.

In engineering inspection of railroad subsystem, traditional engineering analyses have focused on exact expectations for the partitions under mechanical engineering and those under civil engineering. The composite analysis would furnish associations and correlations between partitions under mechanical and civil engineering by further analysis with renewed techniques against big data.

2 Geographical Gathering Procedure of Big Sensor-Data

The data collected from physical world has errors with the sensor employed. In the work of a Worldwide sensor Web[1], the original data is trimmed by abstractions such as table, function, user-defined functions, or model-based views. Data is also subject to noise, and thus data filtering/cleansing is the first phase in the big data analysis.

Before collecting sensor data of the entity from the physical world, the data model should be established for the entity. Data collected from partitions are managed in accordance with their dependencies in the entity. Fig. 1 illustrates the data gathering procedure.

1. Collecting raw data into Data Bunches

Sensor data are measured and collected at the inspection vehicle with inspection instruments. A simple filtering is applied to the collected data and the filtered data is preserved in the moving storage.

2. Copy data bunches to Local Storage

The preserved data of the moving storage are retrieved and copied to a local storage of the Cloud. The retrieved data are copied through simplified classification and extraction.

3. Transferring data bunches to Global Storage

The copied data are filtered and cleansed in the local storage. The data are transferred to the big data storage before their computations.

Once transferred to the Cloud, the data are analyzed with respective techniques in engineering. Since a number of research engineers conduct engineering analyses on respective partitions, a common ontology against the entity is required for semantics shared among research engineers. A semantic Web technology[2] is adopted for provenance of each engineering analysis, in the ontology construction of the entity, for the identification of objects, and in the management of the engineer group.

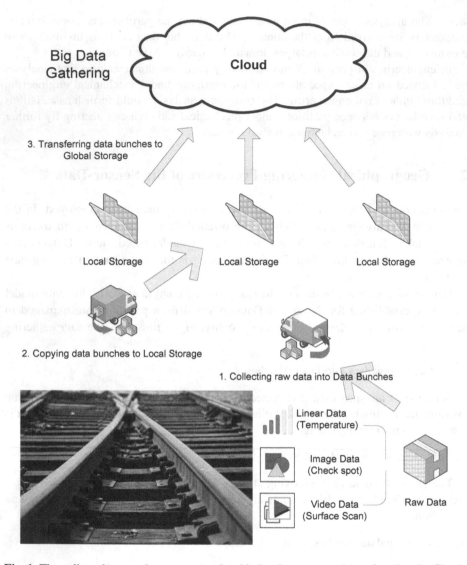

Fig. 1. The collected sensor data are accumulated in local storages and transferred to the Cloud

3   Composite Analysis Procedure on Big Sensor-Data

The traditional engineering analysis is conducted by individual research engineer appropriate to the partition of interest, and the analysis result is input as a context. These contexts could be used for the contextual search after the big data analysis, as those who search for data adequate to the query of complex semantics are research engineers. SOCRADES[3] integration architecture has a similar objective to our ones except that it provides functionalities of embedded devices than sensor data collected out of parts of the partition.

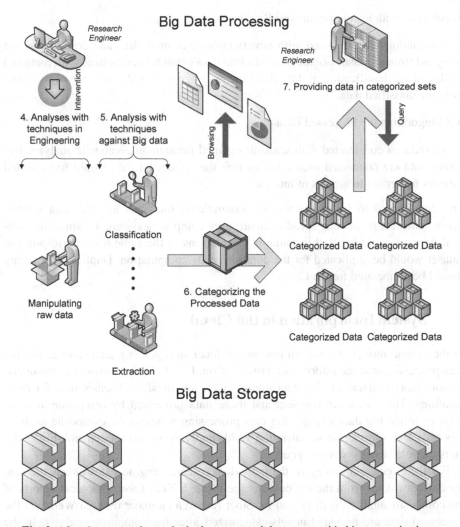

Fig. 2. After the composite analysis the processed data are provided in categorized sets

When the data transferred to the big data storage for their computations, they are duplicated for computation efficiency. The whole data is aggregated with local storages, and only processed results reside on the big data storage. Fig. 2 illustrates the composite analysis procedure.

4. Analyses with techniques in Engineering

Individual research engineer downloads the datasets of a partition and receives notes on inspection conditions(method of inspection, resolution and rate, environment description, and etc.). The person analyzes the datasets with proprietary analysis tools and save the analysis result so that the result could be included in the big data analysis.

5. Analysis with techniques against Big Data

Associations are analyzed with structured/unstructured data and correlations are analyzed from the associations. Searches into data could be parallelized with metadata produced by classification of data along the heterogeneity and extraction of metadata from the classified data.

6. Categorizing the Processed Data

An index is constructed with semantics gained throughout composite analysis. Relevant data are connected each other so that the connected data would form virtual datasets according to aspects of interest.

The data copied to local storages are accumulated for years and the data volume overwhelms the processing speed of an ordinary computing system[4]. Since the identical data set could be used in multiple calculations in the same time, correspondent dataset would be duplicated for the duration of its computation. Duplication strategy should be deliberated for the Cloud.

4   System Incorporation in the Cloud

In the system model, the system consists of local storages, big data storage, the big data processing and the information visualization. Local storages possess accumulated sensor data(raw data) and big data storage manages transferred sensor data for computations. These data are transient and those data processed by composite analysis remains in the big data storage. Big data processing is where the composite analysis proceeds and information visualization yields analysis reports on demand. Fig. 3 depicts the role based system diagram.

For the engineering analysis, the individual research engineer downloads the sensor data(raw data) from the big data storage through FTP. Later, graphical reports of the composite analysis is displayed for other research engineer through Web, and the processed data are provided in sets categorized after the composite analysis. In the engineering analyses, research engineers book respective partitions of the entity. Then the datasets of the partition are transferred to the big data storage and the research engineer is notified. Then these datasets are analyzed with respective techniques in engineering. This process resembles the book-loan one, and the framework in an IOT fashion[5] is adopted in the process of the engineering analysis.

The big data storage manages sensor data transferred from local storages. The transferred data are duplicated for computation efficiency. While duplicating the data, files are treated not to spread widely on many storage devices. The storage manager employs an advanced DHT-based distributed file system, D2[6] for this purpose. The feature of narrowly spread files has an additional benefit in system maintenance.

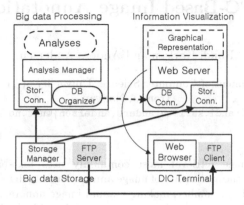

Fig. 3. System Diagram of DIC: The DIC terminal shows graphical reports of the analysis

5   Summary

In the composite analysis, big data analysis is influenced by domain knowledge enlarged with the contexts of each engineering analysis result. The graphical report of the composite analysis is displayed for other research engineer. Therefore the information visualization of the graphical report is of another importance in this work. We consider *Infographics* for information visualization, which is still undergoing. An inforgraphics library would be built in proportion to the number of categories. Visual analytics could be applied in big data analysis for information visualization.

For deep insight through big data analysis, some domain parameters derived from the context could be other key in big data analysis in addition to extracted metadata. The way the engineering analysis result would be input as a context demands a new discussion and it would be discussed in the future work.

References

1. Balazinska, M., Deshpande, A., Franklin, M.J., Gibbons, P.B., Gray, J., Nath, S., Hansen, M., Liebhold, M., Szalay, A., Tao, V.: Data Management in the Worldwide Sensor Web. IEEE Pervasive Computing 6(2), 30–40 (2007)
2. Zhao, J., Wroe, C., Goble, C., Stevens, R., Quan, D., Greenwood, M.: Using Semantic Web Technologies for Representing E-science Provenance. In: McIlraith, S.A., Plexousakis, D., van Harmelen, F. (eds.) ISWC 2004. LNCS, vol. 3298, pp. 92–106. Springer, Heidelberg (2004)
3. Guinard, D., Trifa, V., Karnouskos, S., Spiess, P., Savio, D.: Interacting with the SOA-Based Internet of Things: Discovery, Query, Selection, and On-Demand Provisioning of Web Services. IEEE Transactions on Services Computing 3(3), 223–235 (2010)
4. Jacobs, A.: The Pathologies of Big Data. Communications of the ACM 52(8), 36–44 (2009)
5. Giner, P., Cetina, C., Fons, J., Pelechano, V.: Developing Mobile Workflow Support in the Internet of Things. IEEE Pervasive Computing 9(2), 18–26 (2010)
6. Pang, J., Gibbons, P.B., Kaminsky, M., Seshan, S., Yu, H.: Defragmenting DHT-based Distributed File Systems. In: Proc. International Conference on Distributed Computing Systems, p. 14. IEEE (2007)

NFC-Based Image Annotation

Randi Karlsen and Anders Andersen

Department of Computer Science, University of Tromsø,
Tromsø, Norway
{randi.karlsen,anders.andersen}@uit.no

Abstract. Image retrieval most commonly uses text-based search, which requires the availability of image annotations. As digital photos are growing rapidly in number, making manual image annotation impractical, the need for automatic image annotation is evident. While current approaches to automatic image annotation is based on analysis and interpretation of visual image features and/or image metadata, we present a novel approach to image annotation based on the use of NFC technology. Through a simple touch of an NFC tag, an image capture application obtains accurate annotation information that is automatically added to images. The paper describes how images are associated to the correct NFC tag, enabling a single tag scan to facilitate automatic annotation of multiple images. We also describe how NFC-provided annotations can be used for obtaining more image relevant information from sources on the Internet.

Keywords: Image annotation, NFC-based image annotation, NFC technology, Collecting image information.

1 Introduction

As an enormous amount of digital photos are currently available, an important challenge is to manage them so that relevant photos can be found and displayed in an effective manner. Text-based image retrieval (TBIR) is today the most common technique for searching images [1, 2]. TBIR allows users to formulate high-level semantic queries, and are often more accurate and efficient in identifying relevant images compared to content-based image retrieval (CBIR) [3–5]. However, the technique requires the availability of image annotations (such as tags, description and/or title) that reflect image content. As manual annotation of images is time consuming and impractical due to the huge amount of images [5, 6], solutions for automatic annotation of images are needed. Additionally, automatic annotation may also be needed since people do not necessarily know or remember the names of all depicted objects (for instance attractions visited during a holiday).

Automatic image annotation has received a lot of attention during the last years. Many tools for automatic and semi-automatic annotation use content-based image retrieval (CBIR) techniques for linking visual features to keywords [5, 7]. However, despite the achievements in CBIR, bridging the semantic gap

M. Matera and G. Rossi (Eds.): MobiWIS 2013 Workshops, CCIS 183, pp. 72–85, 2013.

between low-level visual features and high-level semantic concepts is still a challenging task [3, 8]. In addition, CBIR techniques often suffer from low efficiency and scalability caused by the high dimensionality of visual features [5, 9]. Some resent approaches to automatic image annotation combine content analysis techniques with the use of image metadata, such as GPS position, to locate related images on the Web from which annotations can be collected [10–15].

Common to all automatic image annotation techniques, is that annotations are inferred and assigned to an image after analysis of image features and/or image metadata, and based on a probability that the selected annotations are relevant for the image. The accuracy of the techniques vary, and depend on many aspects, for instance the choice of annotation model and how well it can bridge the semantic gap between image features/metadata and semantic image content.

To enable accurate image annotation, we present a novel approach where NFC technology on an Android based cellular phone is used to provide a photo capturing application that automatically adds NFC-provided information as annotation to images. When taking images of an attraction or event, the user obtains image annotations by simply scanning an NFC tag related to the attraction/event. The NFC tag provides a URI that the application uses to contact a server and download textual information that is automatically added as metadata to the images.

This paper describes the photo capture application NfcAnnotate that annotate pictures with data from NFC tags. An important part of this application, is our solution to the challenging task of associating images to the correct NFC tag. We also describe an application for registering image annotations in a supporting backend server, and we describe how NFC-provided annotations can be used for obtaining more image relevant information from sources on the Internet.

2   Background

2.1   Automatic Image Annotation

Automatic and semi-automatic image annotation is the focus in a number of publications, which describe different approaches to selecting textual terms from semantically labeled image samples or previously annotated images. Much work has been done on annotating based on content analysis of images, where machine learning techniques are used to develop image annotation systems that map low-level visual features of an image to high-level concepts [5, 7, 16, 17].

A number of systems annotate a query image by selecting terms from related images gathered from online image collections, such as Flickr[1] and Panoramio[2], based on a combination of geographic position and visual similarity [10–15]. The general technique is to first collect a set of images within a certain radius of the query image, narrow down the set by using visual similarity techniques, and finally collect terms from the remaining images.

---

[1] http://www.flickr.com/
[2] http://www.panoramio.com/

Expansion of user provided image keywords is described in the work of [4, 18–22]. Existing keyword(s) of the image to be annotated, are used in a search that retrieves related images from which candidate terms can be collected. New terms, recommended as expansions, are selected based on visual similarity between images and/or co-occurrence analysis of tags.

Automatic image tagging in mobile phone applications is described in [23–25]. The work in [23, 24] suggest location tags to photos based on information such as location, previously used tags, tags from social contacts and temporal information, while [25] focuses on identifying people in an image by using sensors that detect for instance movement and direction.

The work of [26] describes an early attempt to an NFC-based tourist application and gives a high-level description of a ticketing and photo annotation system. The paper is of a general nature, and does not convey how images are associated with the NFC provided information.

While most of the referred work infer image annotation based on analysis of image visual features and/or image metadata, our approach offers accurate image annotation through the use NFC technology. We provide an new approach in automatic image annotation, where the upcoming NFC technology for tagging our environment, conveniently can be used to add exact annotations to images, and thus avoid interpretations and possible selection of wrongful annotations. In our work we focus on the important issue of how images and NFC-provided annotations are associated. A detailed description of a prototype for NFC-based image annotation is also given.

2.2   NFC and Information Services

NFC Technology. Near field communication (NFC) is a set of short range wireless technologies in family with RFID [27]. It is limited to distances below 10 cm (typically 4cm). This short range is a feature of NFC and not a limitation. The short range can be used to provide context information (presence, selection etc.) and might also be a security feature. NFC provides different bandwidths for communication in the range from 106 kbit/s to 424 kbit/s. NFC communication involves an initiator and a target. The initiator generates an RF field than can power a passive target. Therefore NFC targets do not need a built in power source and can take simple form factors (stickers, key fobs, cards).

NFC tags contain data either custom encoded or using an NFC Forum[3] tag type specification. Data on NFC tags can be typed using MIME types, URI types, or other type specifications. Three NFC operating modes have been defined. In *reader/writer* mode the initiator can read and write data to NFC tags. In *card emulation* mode a card is emulated. This can be a credit card, a key card, tickets or similar. A typical example is a mobile phone emulating a credit card for touch-less payment where the details of this card is stored on a secure element on the phone (e.g. the SIM card). The final operating mode is *peer-to-peer*. In this mode two NFC devices are communicating as peers. A typical example

---

[3] http://www.nfc-forum.org/

is two mobile phones interacting using NFC. In this paper the reader/writer operating mode is used to annotate images.

NFC-Based Information Services. Many information providing applications using the reader/writes NFC mode has been developed [28]. In its most basic usage, data is collected from the NFC tag and displayed on the screen of the mobile device, while in more advanced applications the receiving of information triggers additional processing or delivery of user provided information [28]. Examples of some information providing applications include smart poster applications [29], touch and interact [30], location-based wikis [31] and mobile museum guides [32].

The work of [29] describes an NFC-based solution that helps users finding locations of interest points within a city and navigate to them. Smart Posters are disseminated in the city and provide text and visual information corresponding to the places where they are located. [30] describes an interaction technique that combines mobile phones and public displays. A mesh of NFC tags forms a display, and interaction takes place by touching the display with a phone to read information from a tag. Discussion of a location-based mobil wiki is done in [31], where a touch of an NFC tag should let the user not only open a web page, but also create mobile and local content in the context where they are. A final application example is a mobile guide that uses the interaction with a dynamic NFC-display to let users explore a museum [32].

Current and potential applications of NFC in tourism are reviewed in [33]. These includes, among others, applications like the ones described in [29–32]. Many field trials testing NFC technology, have recently been conducted, and [33] refers to some of the trials where tourist information is provided through NFC technology. Examples are testing done in the city of Nice, at the ski resort Vail (Colorado), at the Museum of London and Google field trials in three cities in the United States.

NFC-based tourist applications are of specific interest in our context, as they demonstrate the interest in a community to use NFC technology to provide people with information about points-of-interest, attractions and events. We believe that a next step in many cases could be to provide information useful for NFC-based tagging of images, as described in this paper.

3   NFC-Based Image Annotation

This chapter presents an NFC-based image annotation application, named Nfc-Annotate, that captures photos and associates them with textual annotations collected through scanning of NFC tags. The application also displays the photos with annotations, and allows the user to change image metadata or simply delete the image.

3.1   NfcAnnotate Architecture

The architecture for NFC-based image tagging, shown in Figure 1, includes two parts, where the lower left part displays the process of registering image annotation information in a backend system and writing a corresponding URI to the NFC tag. The upper right part displays the activity of scanning NFC tags and taking images. In our system, we assume NFC tags with low storage capacity, where only a URI to the backend system is stored on the tag. All annotations for an image are thus collected from the backend system by following the URI.

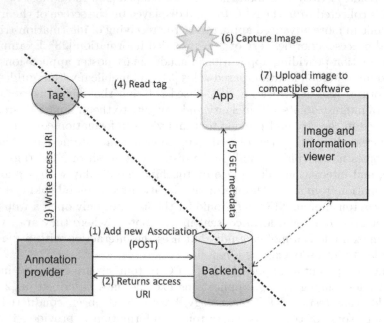

Fig. 1. Architecture of NFC-based image annotation

Registering image annotation information for an attraction or event is first done by filling in a form with the appropriate information and posting it to the backend system. The backend system stores the information and responds with a URI that is subsequently written to an (or a number of) NFC tag(s) that are located at/on the specific attraction or event. The backend system can hold information about a number of attractions and events, each uniquely identified with a URI.

A user with the NfcAnnotate application stored on a mobile device can, before or after taking an image, scan an NFC tag holding information about the captured attraction/event. The URI on the NFC tag is used for collecting image annotation information from the backend system, and the information is stored as metadata on the image. If a connection to the backend system is not available, NfcAnnotate stores the URI on the image, making it possible to later download the annotations.

Images can also be uploaded to some compatible computer software (via wifi or Bluetooth), where they can be displayed and managed. For this, we are currently using the InfoAlbum system [34], that displays images together with information relevant to the image, such as annotations, Wikipedia articles, Web pages, and other images of the same attraction. If the URI is available on the image, InfoAlbum communicates with the backend system to obtain image annotations. InfoAlbum is additionally capable of collecting more image relevant information from various sources in the Internet based on the NFC-provided annotations and other image metadata.

3.2 Associating Tags and Images

To enable NFC-based image annotation, an NFC tag must be scanned and information about the attraction/event, subsequently collected from the backend system. A main challenge, however, is to associate an image with the correct tag.

A number of images can be taken of the same attraction or event, and we do not want to scan the tag each time an image is taken. One scan and multiple tag-image associations must be possible. Also, the tag might be scanned before or after image capture, and there might be a significant time gap between scan and capture. Finally, as there will never be an NFC tag for every image motif, some images will not have an image-tag association.

Formally, we describe the image-tag associations as $\{o, t\}$, where o is an image and t is an NFC tag. If an image o is not part of an image-tag association, this is denoted $\{o, -\}$. The URI on tag t is used to obtain a set of terms, $\{term_1, \ldots, term_n\}$, that are subsequently stored as annotations on o.

An image group $O = \{o_1, \ldots, o_n\}$ represents a group of images that are related to the same attraction/event, and can be associated as a group to an NFC tag, i.e. $\{O, t\}$. This means that all images in O will be given the same set of annotation terms.

An image group is in our system a set of continuously captured images. By scanning an NFC tag t, an image group is (in most cases) started, and every image taken until the group is ended, are associated with tag t. The group is ended (and a new started) when a new tag is scanned. The application also gives the user the option to manually end the group.

To allow for situations where images of an attraction are taken before the tag is scanned, and for taking images that are not associated with any tags, we use a combination of NFC tag scanning and user participation to identify image groups. In Figure 2a we see the image management interface of NfcAnnotate, with buttons (i.e. *Change* and *Stop*) for starting and ending groups.

Table 1 shows the start/end group activities, and the resulting image grouping and associations. In addition to the images-tag association $\{O, t\}$, we use the *Undefined association* $\{O, -\}$ and the *None association* $\{O, N\}$. The Undefined association is used when the photographer wants to add NFC-based annotations to the images, but a tag has not yet been scanned, while the None association is used when an image group has ended without a tag scan.

From Table 1 we see that if an image group O is started with a scan of tag t, the association $\{O, t\}$ is immediately stored. This image group remains active, meaning that new images are added to the group, until a new tag is scanned or the Change or Stop button is pushed. Scanning a tag t having an active group

Table 1. Image group - tag association when starting and ending image groups

Activity	Situation	Image grouping	Association
	no active group	start group O	$\{O, t\}$
Touch tag t	active group, $\{O_1, t'\}$	end group O_1,start group O_2	$\{O_1, t'\}$ $\{O_2, t\}$
	active group, $\{O, -\}$	continue group O_1	$\{O, t\}$
	no active group	start group O	$\{O, -\}$
Push Change	active group, $\{O_1, t'\}$	end group O_1,start group O_2	$\{O_1, t'\}$ $\{O_2, -\}$
	active group, $\{O, -\}$	end group O_1,start group O_2	$\{O_1, N\}$ $\{O_2, -\}$
	no active group	nothing happens	$-$
Push Stop	active group, $\{O, t\}$	end group O	$\{O, t\}$
	active group, $\{O, -\}$	end group O	$\{O, N\}$

O_1 associated with tag t', i.e. $\{O_1, t'\}$, results in the end of group O_1 and start of group O_2 with association $\{O_2, t\}$.

Pushing the Change button, ends an active group and starts a new group with an undefined association, i.e. $\{O, -\}$. A following tag scan, does not start a new group, but will rather identify the association $\{O, t\}$ and continue the current group. If the Change button is pushed once again without a scan of a tag, the association is changed to None, $\{O, N\}$. The relation between images in O are kept, as they are grouped and belonging to the same, undefined topic. The user can later assign annotations to the set of images.

The *Stop* button ends a group without starting a new one. The following images will not be grouped and there will be no association to any tag. This is useful when the next image(s) will not be related to an NFC tagged attraction/event.

3.3   Managing and Displaying Images on the Phone

The NfcAnnotate application allows users to capture, manage and display images taken when using the application. Figure 2 shows two screen shots from NfcAnnotate, one presenting the interface for images management and the second giving an example of how an image is displayed on the mobile device.

In Figure 2a we see, in addition to the Change and Stop button for grouping images, that the user can list previously captured images, upload images to compatible software on a computer, and access settings for the application. The last button *capture photo* is used for activating the camera and taking photos.

Figure 2b shows how an image with associated information is displayed. At the top of the screen, available images are presented as a list, where an image can be chosen for display. Belove, one of the images is displayed, together with image annotations and other metadata, such as name of attraction, textual terms, GPS coordinates and time of capture.

The application stores annotation information for each NFC tag that is scanned. This allows users to manually associate image groups and tags. An NFC tag is often placed on or near the attraction or event for which information is provided. However, one also finds NFC tags on posters (located far away from

 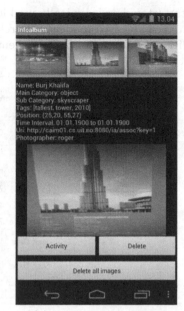

(a) Image management   (b) Displaying an image

Fig. 2. NfcAnnotate interfaces on mobile device

the attraction) and even in brochures (that can be read long before exploring the attractions). The user can in these cases scan a number of tags, that are subsequently stored on the device. When later taking images of an attraction, the user can group images using the NfcAnnotate interface and assign the proper tags to the group.

NfcAnnotate uses NFC tags that are linked to a remote backend system holding annotation information. It has been pointed out that contacting to a remote server may be expensive, especially for foreign users, because of high data roaming charges in many countries [33]. In our application we avoid such costs by storing the URI on the image and collecting annotations when connected to wifi. Also when NFC tags with more storage capacity are used, the annotation information can be stored directly on the tag, making access to a backend system unnecessary.

3.4 NFC Tag Information Registering

To register annotation information on NFC tags, we have implemented a client application with a user interface as shown in Figure 3. In the name field, the user will typically give the exact name of the attraction or event, and then provide three descriptive terms. It is also possible to add GPS latitude and longitude values and a start/stop date. A GPS position gives the exact location of the attraction/event, and can later be used to retrieve other context related material such as location names or images taken by other persons in the same area. A start/stop date is typically used for events that take place within a time-interval, and can be used to focus a search for more information about the event. Such additional information is in our environment provided by the InfoAlbum software that is described in Section 4.

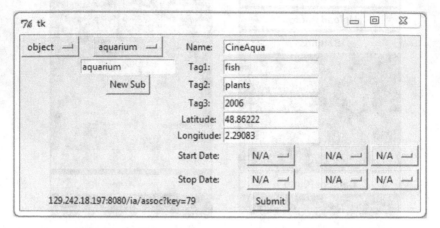

Fig. 3. Specification of annotations for an attraction

In addition to name and terms, the system allows for specifying the general nature of the attraction/event. This means that the user identifies if the annotation information describes an object (i.e. some attraction/point-of-interest) or an event. The user also gives a general description of the attraction/event by categorizing it, for example as a "church", "bridge", "tower", "concert" or "festival". The example in Figure 3 shows that the attraction named CineAqua is described as an "aquarium" of type "object".

All information provided by the user is uploaded to the backend system, and a URI is returned. Next, the URI is written to NFC tag(s) and made available to the public user.

4   Image Information Album as Supporting Application

The NfcAnnotate application allows users to upload images to a supporting application where images and image related information can be displayed on a computer. For this purpose, we have used the InfoAlbum system [34], which presents images together with information about image content and the location of image capture. This information includes attraction/event name, terms, location names, temperature and weather condition at image capture time, placement on map, geographically nearby images, Wikipedia articles, and web pages. Some of the information, such as attraction/event name and terms, are provided by the NfcAnnotate application. The other information is automatically collected by InfoAlbum, from available sources on the Internet, based on image metadata.

The accurate image annotation provided by NfcAnnotate, including name of the attraction/event and GPS coordinates, is very useful metadata that in InfoAlbum is used for expanding with more information. The information automatically collected by InfoAlbum is listed in table 2, where we also see information sources and the metadata needed for obtaining the information.

Table 2. Image relevant information collected by InfoAlbum

Collected information	Source	Metadata
Location names	Flickr	GPS coordinates
Nearby images	Flickr, Panoramio	GPS coordinates
Position on map	Google	GPS coordinates
Weather information	Weather Underground	GPS coordinates, date/time
Wikipedia articles	Wikipedia	Attraction name, Location name
Geo-tagged Wikipedia articles	Wikipedia via GeoNames	GPS coordinates, Attraction name
Web pages	Google	Attraction name, Location name, date/time

Given an image of interest o, *location names* (i.e. country, county and locality), *position on map* and *nearby images* taken by others are all collected based on the GPS coordinates of o, while *weather information* is obtained from Weather Underground[4], by first finding the closest weather station based on latitude and longitude values, and secondly by finding historic information based on the date of image capture and ID of the weather station.

Wikipedia articles are obtained through search on Wikipedia[5] directly, based on attraction and location names, and through searching geo-tagged articles kept by Geonames[6]. GPS coordinates and a radius of interest are input to Geonames, which returns references to Wikipedia articles. Attraction name is then used to identify (if available) the article describing the attraction depicted in the image. Finally, *Web pages* are collected through a Google search, using attraction name and location name as search query. For events images, a time period of interest is additionally used when searching information about the event.

In [34] we reported on testing of InfoAlbum and its ability to collect relevant web pages based on image metadata. In that previous work, exact attraction/event name were not available, but the system rather based the information search on a user provided category keyword, similar to the category information in NfcAnnotator. With the use of NfcAnnotate, attraction/event name is now easily available, and is, not surprisingly, very useful as basis for collecting more relevant information.

In a new test, we compared InfoAlbum results using NfcAnnotate annotations as basis for collecting web pages, to the previous testing where only category

---

[4] http://www.wunderground.com/

[5] http://www.wikipedia.org

[6] http://www.geonames.org/

information were available. The results show that the average precision score increased from 0.43 to 0.91 with the use of NFC-based annotations. The test was based on 50 attraction images, where InfoAlbum executed, for each image, a textual search in Google, filtered the results against a filter list and presented the 20 top ranked web pages to the user. A filtering technique was implemented to ensure that repeatedly occurring, irrelevant web pages were not presented to the user.

5   Discussion

Our approach to NFC-based image annotation combines NFC-tag scanning with the possibility for user participation to determine image-tag associations. This approach brings both opportunities and limitation.

The approach has the advantage of allowing the user to group images as the user finds best. The ability to group images is useful also when NFC-tagging is not available. In such cases, the user can start and end the image group using the NfcAnnotate application and in one operation attach custom tags to all images in a group.

The grouping of successively captured images may well result in a number of groups that associates to the same tag. This may happen if the user switches between topics, for instance while visiting an attraction, described through some tag t, first takes some photos of the attraction, then some images of family members and/or landscape, and continue with more images of the attraction. To automatically associate tag t with both groups, the tag must be scanned twice. Alternatively, the user can manually associate one of the groups with t, since the tag is scanned and stored by the NfcAnnotate application.

On the other hand, the option for user interaction may complicate the process of taking images, in that the user may need to actively start and/or end image grouping. The user must also be aware of how images are grouped, and that for instance a change of topic may require a manual end of group.

Before implementing our current version of NfcAnnotate, we considered using automatic grouping of images based on closeness in location and time between images, and closeness between images and NFC tag. We found, however, that it may be difficult to determine threshold values for both time and distance, since in many cases multiple attractions are located very close and that two images of different attraction may consequently be close both in time and space.

Our approach could also be supplemented by content analysis of images, where similar images can be grouped together [3]. However, in our case we expect visually dissimilar images to be grouped together, as an attraction can be photographed from different angles, outside and inside, and that photos of different artifacts can be part of the group. This makes it very challenging to rely on content-based analysis of images, and this possibility was consequently also discarded for the current implementation of NfcAnnotate.

Based on these considerations, we decided for an approach where users have the possibility to effect the grouping of images, and also provide their own tags if

NFC-tagging is not available. This to avoid the uncertainty introduced by more sophisticated techniques, and the possibility of incorrect image grouping.

6 Conclusion

We have in this paper described a novel method for automatic image annotation using NFC technology. When taking a photo with an Android based mobil device, the NfcAnnotate application enables image annotation by simply letting the user scan an NFC tag that holds information about the attraction or event depicted in the image. The paper described how images of the same attraction/event are grouped and associated with the proper NFC tags, so that a single tag scan can facilitate automatic annotation of multiple images.

This method provides the user with accurate image annotations (such as attraction or event name and GPS coordinates), and is not relying on interpretations or mappings from visual features or image metadata. Annotation information is registered once by an information provider (such as a travel agency or attraction owner), stored in a backend system, and can be fetched by mobile devices running the NfcAnnotate application, using the URI information read from the NFC tag.

This paper also described a supporting application, named infoAlbum, where the annotated images can be displayed and where NFC-provided annotations are used as a basis for collecting more relevant information from sources on the Internet. Additional information provided by InfoAlbum includes Wikipedia articles, Web pages, location names, weather information, placement on map and other images of the same attraction/event. Testing showed that the accurate NFC-provided annotations (such as name of attraction/event and GPS coordinates) represents a very good basis for collecting additional relevant information to the images.

Acknowledgments. The authors appreciate support from the Norwegian Research Council, NFR, through project nr. 176858, Context-aware Image Management, CAIM. We also would thank the student Roger Bruun Asp Hansen for contributing to the implementation of NfcAnnotate.

References

1. Pagare, R., Shinde, A.: A Study on Image Annotation Techniques. International Journal of Computer Applications 37(6) (January 2012)
2. Sergieh, H.M., et al.: Geo-based Automatic Image Annotation. In: Proceedings of the 2nd ACM International Conference on Multimedia Retrieval, ICMR 2012, Hong Kong, China (June 2012)
3. Datta, R., Joshi, D., Li, J., Wang, J.Z.: Image retrieval: Ideas, influences, and trends of the new age. ACM Computing Survey 40(2), Article 5 (April 2008)
4. Wu, L., Jin, R., Jain, A.: Tag Completion for Image Retrieval. IEEE Transactions on Pattern Analysis and Machine Intelligence (May 2012)

5. Zhang, D., Islam, M., Lu, G.: A review on automatic image annotation techniques. Pattern Recognition 45(1) (2012)
6. Whittaker, S., Bergman, O., Clough, P.: Easy on that trigger dad: a study of long term family photo retrieval. Personal Ubiquitous Computing 14(1) (January 2010)
7. Wang, M., et al.: Assistive Tagging: A Survey of Multimedia Tagging with Human-Computer Joint Exploration. ACM Computing Surveys 44(4) (2012)
8. Smeulders, A.W.M., et al.: Content-Based Image Retrieval at the End of the Early Years. IEEE Transactions on Pattern Analysis and Machine Intelligence 22(12) (December 2000)
9. Wang, C., et al.: Scalable Search-Based Image Annotation of Personal Images. In: Proceedings of the 8th ACM SIGMM International Workshop on Multimedia Information Retrieval, MIR 2006, Santa Barbara, CA, USA, October 26-27 (2006)
10. Jones, G.J.F., Byrne, D., Hughes, M., O'Connor, N.E., Salway, A.: Automated Annotation of Landmark Images Using Community Contributed Datasets and Web Resources. In: Declerck, T., Granitzer, M., Grzegorzek, M., Romanelli, M., Rüger, S., Sintek, M. (eds.) SAMT 2010. LNCS, vol. 6725, pp. 111–126. Springer, Heidelberg (2011)
11. Joshi, D., et al.: Using Geotags to Derive Rich Tag-Clouds for Image Annotation. In: Social Media Modeling and Computing. Springer London (2011)
12. Mousselly, H., et al.: Geo-based Automatic Image Annotation. In: Proceeding of the ACM International Conference on Multimedia Retrieval (ICMR 2012), Hong Kong, China (June 2012)
13. Moxley, E., Kleban, J., Manjunath, B.: Spirittagger: A Geo-Aware Tag Suggestion Tool Mined from Flickr. In: Proceeding of the 1st ACM International Conference on Multimedia Information Retrieval, MIR 2008, Vancouver, Canada (October 2008)
14. Popescu, A., Moëllic, P.A.: MonuAnno: automatic annotation of georeferenced landmarks images. In: Proceeding of the ACM International Conference on Image and Video Retrieval, CIVR 2009, Island of Santorini, Greece (July 2009)
15. Silva, A., Martins, B.: Tag recommendation for georeferenced photos. In: Proceedings of the 3rd ACM SIGSPATIAL International Workshop on Location-Based Social Networks (LBSN 2011). ACM, New York (2011)
16. Makadia, A., Pavlovic, V., Kumar, S.: Baselines for Image Annotation. International Journal of Computer Vision 90(1) (2010)
17. Tsai, C.-F., Hung, C.: Automatically Annotating Images with Keywords: A Review of Image Annotation Systems. In: Recent Patents on Computer Science, vol. 1. Bentham Science Publishers (2008)
18. Gao, S., et al.: Automatic image tagging via category label and web data. In: Proceedings of the International Conference on Multimedia (MM 2010). ACM, New York (2010)
19. Wang, X.-J., et al.: AnnoSearch: Image Auto-Annotation by Search, in. In: Proceedings of the 2006 IEEE Computer Society Conference on Computer Vision and Pattern Recognition, vol. 2. IEEE Computer Society Press (2006)
20. Kucuktunc, O., Sevil, S.G., Tosun, A.B., Zitouni, H., Duygulu, P., Can, F.: Tag suggestr: Automatic photo tag expansion using visual information for photo sharing websites. In: Duke, D., Hardman, L., Hauptmann, A., Paulus, D., Staab, S. (eds.) SAMT 2008. LNCS, vol. 5392, pp. 61–73. Springer, Heidelberg (2008)
21. Rae, A., Sigurbjörnsson, B., van Zwol, R.: Improving tag recommendation using social networks. In: 9th International Conference on Adaptivity, Personalization and Fusion of Heterogeneous Information (RIAO 2010), Paris, France (2010)

22. Sigurbjörnsson, B., van Zwol, R.: Flickr tag recommendation based on collective knowledge. In: Proceedings of the 17th International Conference on World Wide Web (WWW 2008). ACM, New York (2008)
23. Ahern, S., et al.: Zonetag: Designing context-aware mobile media capture to increase participation. In: Proceeding of the Pervasive Image Capture and Sharing Workshop (PICS), Orange County, California (September 2006)
24. Naaman, M., Nair, R.: ZoneTag's Collaborative Tag Suggestions: What is This Person Doing in My Phone? IEEE MultiMedia 15(3), 34–40 (2008)
25. Qin, C., et al.: TagSense: A Smartphone-based Approach to Automatic Image Tagging. In: Proceedings of the 9th International Conference on Mobile Systems, Applications and Services, MobiSys 2011, Bethesda, Maryland, USA, June 28-July 1 (2011)
26. Eow, A.S.H., Guo, J., Guan, S.-U.: Tourist Applications Made Easier Using Near Field Communication. In: Pagani, M. (ed.) Encyclopedia of Multimedia Technology and Networking. IGI Global (2009)
27. Ortiz, C.E.: An introduction to near-field communication and the contactless communication API. Tech. rep., Oracle Sun (2008)
28. Ok, K., Coskun, V., Aydin, M.N., Ozdenizci, B.: Current Benefits and Future Directions of NFC Services. In: Proceedings of the International Conference on Education and Management Technology (ICEMT 2010), Cairo, Egypt (November 2010)
29. Borrego-Jaraba, F., Luque Ruiz, I., Gómez-Nieto, M.: A NFC-based pervasive solution for city touristic surfing. Personal Ubiquitous Comput 15(7) (2011)
30. Hardy, R., Rukzio, E.: Touch & Interact: touch-based interaction with a tourist application. In: Proceedings of the 10th International Conference on Human Computer Interaction with Mobile Devices and Services (MobileHCI 2008). ACM, New York (2008)
31. Siira, E., Tuikka, T., Tormanen, V.: Location-Based Mobile Wiki Using NFC Tag Infrastructure. In: Proceedings of the 2009 First International Workshop on Near Field Communication (NFC 2009). IEEE Computer Society, Washington, DC (2009)
32. Blockner, M., et al.: Please touch the exhibits!: using NFC-based interaction for exploring a museum. In: Proceedings of the 11th International Conference on Human-Computer Interaction with Mobile Devices and Services (MobileHCI 2009). ACM, New York (2009)
33. Pesonen, J., Horster, E.: Near field communication technology in tourism. Tourism Management Perspectives 4 (2012)
34. Karlsen, R., Jakobsen, B., Hansen, R.B.: Uncover What You See In Your Images, The InfoAlbum Approach. The International Journal of Computer Science and Applications IX(I) (2012)

Towards QoS in Internet of Things for Delay Sensitive Information

Irfan Awan[1] and Muhammad Younas[2]

[1] Department of Computing,
University of Bradford,
Bradford BD7 1DP, UK
i.u.awan@bradford.ac.uk
[2] Department of Computing and Communication Technologies,
Oxford Brookes University,
Oxford OX33 1HX, UK
m.younas@brookes.ac.uk

Abstract. Ensuring QoS for transmission of delay sensitive information is of paramount importance in network of smart devices formally known as Internet of Things (IoTs). The most commonly used Best Effort service model cannot be an attractive mechanism to treat delay sensitive traffic. Heterogeneous smart devices with limited buffer capacity needs effective buffer management scheme and differentiated service priorities to provide preferential treatment to delay sensitive traffic. This paper proposes a cost-effective analytical model for a finite capacity queueing system with pre-emptive resume service priority and push-out buffer management scheme. The analytical model can be used to predict the performance of smart devices under various traffic conditions that meet the required QoS constraints of IoT devices.

Keywords: Internet of Things, QoS, Modelling, Traffic, delay sensitive.

1   Introduction

The Internet of Things (IoT), that effectively interconnects large number of smart devices (things), creates an environment wherein things have interfaces and identities and can communicate through standard and interoperable communication protocols [1, 2]. IoT is not a standalone network. Instead, it combines various network infrastructures such as sensor networks, wireless networks and standard Internet, in order to retrieve useful information from things, interact with physical world, and provide various services in different application domains such as smart cities [3], supply chain management [4], and healthcare [5] to name a few [7]. In [8], Yang et al describe the motivation and benefits of the use of IoT technologies in emergency management operations and response times. One of the main findings of this work is that "IoT technology provides added value to emergency response operations in terms of obtaining efficient cooperation, accurate situational awareness, and complete visibility

M. Matera and G. Rossi (Eds.): MobiWIS 2013 Workshops, CCIS 183, pp. 86–94, 2013.

of resources". In addition, various large scale research projects have been investigating into IoT and related application areas. For instance, the SmartSantander project (http://www.smartsantander.eu/) investigates into the application areas of IoT such as smart city. They take into account various cities in experimental studies such as Belgrade, Guildford, Lübeck and Santander. Similarly, the IoT6 project (http://www.iot6.eu) investigates into IPv6 in order to design and develop scalable IPv6-based services architecture that enables the integration and interoperation of things, applications and services. Moreover, Web of Things (WoT) models have started to emerge in order to supplement IoT with software services. For instance, the authors in [20] propose a lightweight architecture which is based on RESTful web services. This work uses smart city case study and combines various new software technologies to support the design and development of WoT applications which can use IoT as an underlying network infrastructure.

Generally, in IoT, things are required to be actively participating in various activities, exchanging information and making intelligent decision without much reliance on human involvement [6]. Smart homes are equipped with various intelligent devices to ensure safety, security and high performance of electrical appliances. These devices are usually connected with personal mobile devices through GSM or GPRS. Mobile devices are increasingly being used for Internet browsing, Internet telephony and electronic shopping in addition to its traditional use of voice calls. Mobile devices are equipped with small buffers but have to deal with IoT services that generate a huge volume of data. Thus an effective buffer management scheme together with an appropriate service scheduling mechanism is essential to ensure instant communication without facing any packet loss or queuing delay. A typical example can be an incident of a break into a smart home. An intelligent CCTV camera takes a picture of an intruder and instantly sends a priority message (packet) together with the photograph of the intruder to the home owner's mobile device. In this perspective, it is necessary to design and develop service models that ensure appropriate level of QoS for delay sensitive applications in IoT.

Current approaches provide unsatisfactory solutions for delay-sensitive applications and ignore the key parameters such as deadline, importance of delays, etc. Such problems become more complicated in IoT where communication media and device resources are scarce. This paper focuses on modeling IoT applications that are involved in producing consuming delay sensitive information.

The proposed model/method aims to analyse a finite capacity queue with push-out buffer management scheme and pre-emptive resume (PR) service priority. The cost-effective exact analytical solution for this queue will be used to evaluate the performance of smart devices under varying traffic conditions so as to ensure preferential treatment of highest priority delay sensitive data.

The rest of the paper is structured as follows. Section 2 provides an analysis of the related work. Section 3 designs and develops the proposed model. Section 4 gives an overview of the performance evaluation of the proposed model. Section 5 concludes the paper and identifies directions for future research work.

2   Related Work

IoT deals with all kind of traffic requiring various level of QoS constraints. For example, emergency messages are more sensitive to delay than other types of traffic. Various service scheduling have been proposed (e.g., FCFS, Head of Line, etc) under different buffer management schemes ranging from dedicated buffer access for each class to the shared buffer with space priority. There is only a small number of studies for analyzing service priorities under push-out buffer management. Mostly such studies have been conducted for ATM networks with fixed size cells.

The authors in [7, 9] present surveys on IoT vision, IoT related projects, application and impact areas, enabling technologies and the research issues such as interoperability, privacy, trust, energy and resource scarcity of things in IoT. These are useful surveys and provide high level description of QoS issues but without proposing any model or solution.

Jin et al [3] present four types of network architectures in a smart city, which is one of the potential areas of IoT. These include autonomous network, ubiquitous network, application-layer overlay network and service-oriented network architectures. These network architectures are compared using factors such as design approach, connectivity model, Network hierarchy In-Network Processing, QoS complexity and progress in defining QoS. Though such comparison is very useful the analysis is very abstract and does not provide any in-depth investigation of the QoS issues. Nef et al [6] analyse WSNs integration approaches in the IoT, which are considered to be the main contributors to the IoT QoS. The paper also presents the feasibility and different (best) ways for integrating WSNs into the IoT. The above approaches do not look into the QoS of delay-sensitive applications in IoT.

Kleoec and Kos in [10] present the behaviour of packet transit times for a delay sensitive application with certain minimum bandwidth constraint. They propose a simple model with two queues under priority and FCFS service rules. Both queues work under a complete sharing scheme. Although this model is simple, the utilization of higher priority depends on the delay sensitive traffic intensity and can result in small queue length for high priority traffic at the cost of high data loss for low priority data under low high priority traffic load. The authors in [11] investigate into the impact of buffering under complete buffer sharing scheme on resource allocation in wireless local area networks using heterogeneous traffic loads. The results indicate that, in the presence of heterogeneous loads, 802.11 does not allocate transmission opportunities equally. They show that large buffers can help this inequality at the expense of significantly increased delay which is mainly due to absence of an effective buffering scheme and service priorities. Guo et al [12] introduced an Awareness Driven Schedule (ADS) scheme that enables sensors to provide differentiated data service by their awareness. The higher a sensor resource's awareness on the event is, the more detailed data service it should provide.

Further, various approaches have been developed in order to monitor and analyse network topologies [14], performance related issues [15], and availability of bandwidth [16]. The work in [17] takes into consideration passive and active monitoring techniques, while the works in [18] and [19] respectively deal with workload characterization and the evaluation of QoS/QoE [19].

In summary the above approaches do not give particular attention to the performance analysis of delay sensitive applications in IoT.

3   The Proposed Model

This paper proposes a $[M]^X/M/1/N$ queuing system with pre-emptive resume (PR) service priority and finite capacity queue with complete buffer sharing scheme by all classes of traffic under a push out mechanism. The proposed model can be used to evaluate the performance of smart devices to meet various QoS constraints under varying input parameterization. In the proposed system, it is assumed that the arriving traffic is classified into low priority (normal traffic) and high priority (emergency traffic). The inter-arrival times and service times for each arriving class of traffic are distributed according to exponential distribution. These are modeled as follows.

Let,

- λ_i be the arrival rate of class i traffic, for i=1,2, where class 1 has the highest priority
- μ_i be the service rate for class i traffic, for i=1,2,
- N be the total buffer capacity under complete buffer sharing with push-out mechanism
- $\mathbf{n} = (n_1, n_2, \ldots, n_R)$ be a joint queue state where $\sum_{i=1}^{R} n_i \le N$, R=2
- $P(\mathbf{n})$ be the joint state probabilities

Finite capacity buffer is managed under a complete sharing scheme whilst giving highest priority to emergency traffic signals. Upon arrival to a full buffer, a highest priority class traffic packet will push-out the lower priority class packet. Service scheduling follows PR priority discipline in which higher priority traffic is serviced according to FCFS prior to lower priority traffic. Lower priority traffic is served only in absence of higher priority traffic and is immediately pre-empted upon arrival of emergency data packets — which could also be pushed out if buffer is full in order to avoid data loss of the delay sensitive traffic.

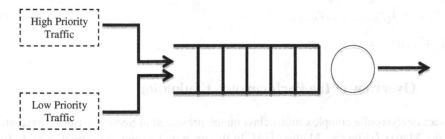

Fig. 1. [M]X/M/1/N queuing system with two classes of traffic and a shared buffer

The two dimensional Markov chain for $[M]^X/M/1/N$ with PR service priority and Push-out buffer management scheme can be constructed as follows:

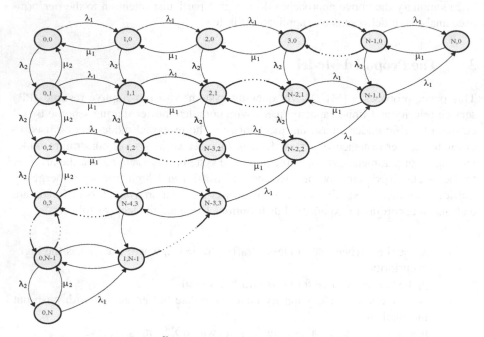

Fig. 2. Markov chain for $[M]^X/M/1/N$ queuing system with PR priority and push-out buffer

The flow balance equations, based on this Markov chain, can be derived as follows:

$$(\lambda_1 + \lambda_2)P_{0,0} = \mu_1 P_{1,0} + \mu_2 P_{0,1} \tag{1}$$

$$(\lambda_1 + \lambda_2 + \mu_1)P_{i,j} = \lambda_1 P_{i-1,j} + \lambda_2 P_{i,j-1} + \mu_1 P_{i+1,j}, \ \forall i \geq 1, j = 0, \tag{2}$$
$$where \ P_{i,-1} = 0$$

$$(\lambda_1 + \lambda_2 + \mu_2)P_{0,j} = \lambda_2 P_{0,j-1} + \mu_2 P_{0,j+1} + \mu_1 P_{1,j}, \forall j \geq 1, \tag{3}$$

$$\mu_1 P_{N,0} = \lambda_1 P_{N-1,0} + \lambda_1 P_{N-1,1} \tag{4}$$

$$(\lambda_1 + \mu_2)P_{0,N} = \lambda_2 P_{0,N-1} \tag{5}$$

4   Overview of the Performance Evaluation

Exact analysis of a complex multi-class queue presented in Section 3 can be evaluated using Matrix Geometric Method [13]. In the proposed model the arrival process follows the Poisson distribution whereas the service times are exponentially distributed.

The Matrix Geometric Method is used to solve the stationary state probability for vector state Markov process. The flow balance equations (1)-(5) can be easily solved using the following relation

$$PQ = 0 \tag{6}$$

where P is a vector of joint state probabilities, represented as

$$P = (P_{0,0}, P_{1,0}, P_{2,0}, \dots, P_{N,0}, P_{0,1}, \dots, P_{0,N})$$

and Q is rate matrix represented as

$$Q = \begin{pmatrix} (\lambda_1 + \lambda_2) & \lambda_2 & \lambda_1 & & & \\ \mu_1 & (\lambda_1 + \lambda_2 + \mu_2) & & \lambda_2 & & \vdots \\ \mu_2 & & (\lambda_1 + \lambda_2 + \mu_1) & & & \\ & \mu_2 & & (\lambda_1 + \lambda_2 + \mu_2) & & \vdots \\ & \mu_1 & 0 & & & \\ & & \mu_1 & & \mu_2 & \\ & & & & \mu_1 & \\ & & & & & \vdots \end{pmatrix}$$

which can be simplified as

$$Q = \begin{pmatrix} A_0 & \Lambda_0 & & & & \\ M_1 & A_1 & \Lambda_1 & & & \\ & M_2 & A_2 & \Lambda_2 & & \\ & & M_3 & A_3 & & \\ & & & & \Lambda_{N-1} \\ & & & M_N & A_N \end{pmatrix} \tag{7}$$

where

$$A_0 = (\lambda_1 + \lambda_2)$$

$$A_1 = \begin{pmatrix} (\lambda 1 + \lambda 2 + \mu 2) & \\ & (\lambda_1 + \lambda_2 + \mu_1) \end{pmatrix}$$

$$A_2 = \begin{pmatrix} (\lambda 1 + \lambda 2 + \mu 2) & & \\ & (\lambda_1 + \lambda_2 + \mu_1) & \\ & & (\lambda_1 + \lambda_2 + \mu_1) \end{pmatrix}$$

...

...

$$\Lambda_0 = (\lambda_2 \quad \lambda_1)$$

$$\Lambda_1 = \begin{pmatrix} \lambda_2 & & \lambda_1 & \\ & \lambda_2 & & \lambda_1 \end{pmatrix}$$

$$\Lambda_2 = \begin{pmatrix} \lambda_2 & & \lambda_1 & \\ & \lambda_2 & & \lambda_1 \\ & & \lambda_2 & \end{pmatrix}$$

...

...

$$M_1 = \begin{pmatrix} \mu_1 \\ \mu_2 \end{pmatrix}$$

$$M_2 = \begin{pmatrix} \mu_2 & & 0 \\ \mu_1 & & \\ & \mu_1 \end{pmatrix}$$

$$M_3 = \begin{pmatrix} \mu2 & & & \\ \mu_1 & & & \\ & \mu_1 & & 0 \\ & & \mu_1 \end{pmatrix}$$

...

...

Using equations (6) and (7), we can derive the following expressions for steady state probabilities:

$$P_N A_N = P_{N-1}\Lambda_{N-1}$$

which can written as

$$P_N = P_{N-1}\Lambda_{N-1}A_N^{-1} \tag{8}$$

Similarly

$$P_{N-1}A_{N-1} = P_{N-2}\Lambda_{N-2} + P_N M_N \tag{9}$$

Substituting P_N from equation (8) into equation (9), gives:

$$P_{N-1} = P_{N-2}\Lambda_{N-2}(A_{N-1} - \Lambda_{N-1}A_N^{-1}M_N)^{-1}$$

$$P_{N-2} = P_{N-3}\Lambda_{N-3}(A_{N-2} - \Lambda_{N-2}A_{N-1}^{-1}M_{N-1})^{-1}$$

and so on.

Using these steady state probabilities, various performance measures can be easily derived such as loss probability, mean waiting times and mean queue length occupancy.

5   Conclusion

This paper highlighted the importance of ensuring the QoS for transmission of delay sensitive information in IoT. It reviewed related work and identified issues related to the QoS in IoT. The paper specifically examined that the most commonly used Best Effort service model cannot provide a proper solution for delay sensitive traffic. There exist a variety of devices in IoT; each having varying but limited capacity for storing, processing and exchanging information with other devices.

In this paper we therefore take account of the characteristics of IoT devices and the importance of delay sensitive information. We proposed a cost-effective analytical model for a finite capacity queueing system with pre-emptive resume service priority and push-out buffer management scheme. The analytical model can be used to predict the performance of smart devices under various traffic conditions that meet the QoS constraints.

References

1. Vermesan, O., et al.: Internet of Things Strategic Research Roadmap. European Research Cluster on the Internet of Things, Cluster Strategic Research Agenda (2011)
2. Kortuem, G., et al.: Educating the Internet-of-Things Generation. Computer 46(2), 53–61 (2013)
3. Jin, J., Gubbi, J., Luo, T., Palaniswami, M.: Network Architecture and QoS Issues in the Internet of Things for a Smart City. In: Proceedings of the 12th International Sym-posium on Communications and Information Technologies (ISCIT 2012), Gold Cost, Australia, pp. 974–979. IEEE (October 2012)
4. Konomi, S., Roussos, G.: Ubiquitous Computing in the Real World: Lessons Learnt from Large-Scale RFID Deployments. Personal and Ubiquitous Computing 11(7), 507–521 (2007)
5. Ghose, A., Bhaumik, C., Das, D., Agrawal, A.K.: Mobile healthcare infrastruc-ture for home and small clinic. In: Proceedings of the 2nd ACM International Workshop on Perva-sive Wireless Healthcare (MobileHealth 2012), pp. 15–20. ACM, New York (2012)
6. Nef, M.-A., Perlepes, L., Karagiorgou, S., Stamoulis, G.I., Kikiras, P.K.: Enabling QoS in the Internet of Things. In: Proceedings of the Fifth International Conference on Communi-cation Theory, Reliability, and Quality of Service (CTRQ 2012), Chamonix / Mont Blanc, France, pp. 33–38 (2012)
7. Atzori, L., Iera, A., Morabito, G.: The Internet of Things: A Survey. Computer Net-works 54(15), 2787–2805 (2010)
8. Yang, L., Yang, S.H., Plotnick, L.: How the Internet of Things Technology En-hances Emergency Response Operations. Technological Forecasting & Social Change (2012), http://dx.doi.org/10.1016/j.bbr.2011.03.031
9. Miorandi, D., Sicari, S., Pellegrini, F.D., Chlamtac, I.: Internet of things: Vision, applica-tions and research challenges. Ad Hoc Networks 10(7), 1497–1516 (2012)

10. Klepec, B., Kos, A.: Performance of VoIP Applications in a Simple Differentiated Services Network Architecture (EUROCON). In: Proceedings of the International Conference on Trends in Communications, Bratislava, Slovakia, vol. 1, pp. 214–217 (2001)
11. Duffy, K., Ganesh, A.J.: Modeling the Impact of Buffering on 802.11. IEEE Communications Letters 11(2), 219–221 (2007)
12. Guo, H., Ma, S., Liang, F.: Enabling Awareness Driven Differentiated Data Service in IoT. Journal of Networks 6(11), 1572–1577 (2011)
13. Neuts, M.: Matrix-geometric solutions in stochastic models: an algorithmic approach. Dover Pubns (1994)
14. Donnet, B., Friedman, T.: Internet topology discovery: A survey. IEEE Communications Surveys & Tutorials 9(4), 56–69 (2007)
15. Cui, H., Biersack, E.: Trouble shooting interactive web sessions in a home environment. In: 2nd ACM SIGCOMM Workshop on Home Networks (2011)
16. Guerrero, C.D., Labrador, M.A.: On the applicability of available bandwidth estimation techniques and tools. Computer Communications 33(1), 11–22 (2010)
17. Botta, A., Dainotti, A., Pescapè, A.: Do You Trust Your Software-based Traffic Generator? IEEE Communications Magazine 48(9), 158–165 (2010)
18. Dainotti, A., Pescape, A., Claffy, K.C.: Issues and future directions in traffic classification. IEEE Network 26(1), 35–40 (2012)
19. Sundaresan, S., de Donato, W., Feamster, N., Teixeira, R., Crawford, S., Pescapè, A.: Broadband internet performance: A view from the gateway. In: Proc. of ACM SIGCOMM, Toronto, Ontario, Canada (August 2011)
20. Grønli, T.-M., Ghinea, G., Younas, M.: A Lightweight Architecture for the Web-of-Things. In: Daniel, F., Papadopoulos, G.A., Thiran, P. (eds.) MobiWIS 2013. LNCS, vol. 8093, pp. 248–259. Springer, Heidelberg (2013)

Modelling Usage Control of a U-Learning System Using CA-UCON

Abdulgader Almutairi and François Siewe

Software Technology Research Laboratory,
De Montfort University,
The Gateway, Leicester, LE1 9BH, UK
{Abdulgader,fsiewe}@dmu.ac.uk

Abstract. A Context-Aware Usage CONtrol (CA-UCON) model is an extension of the traditional UCON model which enables adaptation to environmental changes in the aim of preserving continuity of usage in a pervasive computing system. When the authorisations and obligations requirements are met by the subject and the object, and the conditions requirements fail due to changes in the environment or the system context, CA-UCON model triggers specific actions to adapt to the new situation. Besides the data protection, CA-UCON model so enhances the quality of services, striving to keep explicit interactions with the user at a minimum. In this paper, this model is used to model usage control in a u-learning system and analyse its properties through simulation.

Keywords: Pervasive system, Ubiquitous learning, context-aware, usage control.

1 Introduction

The notion of ubiquitous learning (u-learning) has become more prevalent since the development of new ICT technologies facilitating ubiquitous computing, and since electronic communications have become so widespread [13]. However, the reason behind the recent evolution of u-learning is that there are now increasing demands for different learning methods to solve the challenges of learning in a flexible manner. U-learning is defined as the ability of a ubiquitous computing system to sense the learner's situation and to offer him/her adaptive contents based on his/her context (this is called context-awareness).

U-learning is described as a special case of m-learning, with the notion of learning being based on context. Thus, the aim of u-learning is that it considers the context of the learner in order to provide her/him with learning contents at appropriate times and in appropriate situations. U-learning is similar to m-learning in terms of mobility but u-learning goes beyond m-learning by including a high level of embeddedness. This is because u-learning is able to determine the learner's context using a number of sensors in order to detect and gather information pertaining to the learner and his/her particular environment. As such, security is a major concerns for the acceptance of such systems.

M. Matera and G. Rossi (Eds.): MobiWIS 2013 Workshops, CCIS 183, pp. 95–109, 2013.
© Springer International Publishing Switzerland 2013

Usage CONtrol (UCON) model [4] is the latest major enhancement of the traditional access control models which enables *mutability* of subject and object attributes, and *continuity* of control on usage of resources. While the concept of mutability refers to the fact that attributes are not static but does change intermittently, continuity of access decision ensures that decision to permit and allow access to an object is made constantly before and during the access to an object. This access decision is based on three key factors: authorisations, obligations and conditions. Because of the continuity of access decision, access permission may be revoked as a result of changes in the environmental or system context, regardless of whether the authorisations and obligations requirements are met. This constitutes a major shortcoming of the UCON model in pervasive computing systems which constantly strives to adapt to environmental changes so as to minimise disruptions to the user.

A Context-Aware Usage CONtrol (CA-UCON) model was proposed [1] which extends the traditional UCON model to enable adaptation to environmental changes in the aim of preserving *continuity of usage*. In this paper, we present modelling of usage control in ubiquitous learning system (u-learning)using CA-UCON. Our main contributions are summarised as follows:

- A Modelling of usage control in ubiquitous learning system using CA-UCON model is presented (Sect. 5).
- A validation of ubiquitous learning system properties using CCA execution environment is presented (Sect. 6).

2   Overview of CA-UCON Model

A Context-Aware Usage CONtrol (CA-UCON) model is an extension of the traditional UCON model to enable adaptation to environmental changes in the aim of preserving continuity of access [1]. Indeed, when the authorisations and obligations requirements are met by the subject and the object, and the conditions requirements fail due to changes in the environmental or the system context, CA-UCON model triggers specific actions to adapt to the new situation. Besides the data protection, CA-UCON model so enhances the quality of services, keeping explicit interactions with the user at a minimum. [4] defined the $UCON_{ABC}$ family core models where A stands for Authorisations, B for oBligations and C for Conditions. We defined the $CA\text{-}UCON_{ABD}$ family core models where C is replaced by D for aDaptation. So the $CA\text{-}UCON_A$ and $CA\text{-}UCON_B$ family core models are identical to $UCON_A$ and $UCON_B$, respectively. The $CA\text{-}UCON_D$ family core model comprises two models: the pre-adaptation model $CA\text{-}UCON_{preD}$ and the on-going adaptation model $CA\text{-}UCON_{onD}$, which are detailed below.

2.1   The $CA\text{-}UCON_{preD}$ Model

In the $CA\text{-}UCON_{preD}$ model, adaptation can be activated only before the access permission is granted. That is adaptation cannot take place during access. If s

is subject, o and object and r an access right, we let $preD(s,o,r)$ denote a predicate which is true if the pre-adaptation is successful and false otherwise. We also denote the access permission decision by the predicate $allowed(s, o, r)$. The CA-UCON$_{preD}$ core model is composed of the following elements:

- S: set of subjects, $ATT(S)$: set of subject attributes.
- O: set of objects, $ATT\ (O)$: set of object attributes.
- AD: set of adaptation actions.
- $PreCON$: set of pre-conditions elements.
- T: time domain.
- $PreAdapted : 2^{preCON} \times AD \times T \to \{true, false\}$

 $preAdapted(c,\ a,\ t)$ is a boolean function that performs the adaptation action a until all the conditions in c evaluate to true, in which case the function returns $true$; otherwise the function returns $false$ after t time-units have elapsed since the execution of the action a started.

- $getPreADAPT : S \times O \times R \to 2^{preCON} \times AD \times T$
 $getPreADAPT(s,\ o,\ r)$ returns a tuple $(c,\ a,\ t)$ where c is the set of all pre-conditions required to grant the subject s the access right r upon the object o, a is the adaptation action to be performed if any of the pre-conditions does not hold, and t is the time-out for this adaptation process.

- $getPreAltReq : S \times O \times R \to 2^{O \times R}$

 $getPreAltReq(s,\ o,\ r)$ denotes the set of alternative requests that can be made on behalf of the subject s when the initial request of the access right r upon the object o could not be granted due to environmental conditions.

- $preD(s,\ o,\ r)\ =\ preAdapted(getPreADAPT(s,\ o,\ r\ ))$

- The access permission decision is defined as:

- $allowed(s,o,r) \Rightarrow preD(s,o,r)$;
 This predicate denotes that the subject s is granted the right r to access the object o, if the adaptation process for this access request is successful.

$$ended(s, o, r) \Rightarrow \begin{pmatrix} \neg preD(s,o,r) \\ \wedge \\ \bigvee_{(o',r') \in E} allowed(s, o', r') \end{pmatrix}$$

This predicate denotes that the right r requested by the subject s to access the object o is ended, if the predicate $preD$ is false and an alternative request is issued.

 where $E = getPreAltReq(s, o, r)$ and the symbol '$\Rightarrow$' denotes the logical implication.

2.2   The CA-UCON$_{onD}$ Model

In the CA-UCON$_{onD}$ model, there is no pre-adaptation; adaptation can only take place during access. If s is subject, o and object and r an access right, we let $onD(s, o, r)$ denote a predicate which is true if the on-going adaptation is successful and false otherwise. We also denote by $stopped(s, o, r)$ a predicate which is true if the access has been stopped. The CA-UCON$_{onD}$ core model is composed of the following elements:

- S: set of subjects, $ATT(S)$: set of subject attributes.
- O: set of objects, $ATT\ (O)$: set of object attributes.
- AD: set of adaption strategies (or actions)
- $onCON$: set of ongoing-conditions elements
- T: time domain
- $onAdapted : 2^{onCON} \times AD \times T \rightarrow \{true, false\}$

  $onAdapted(c, a, t)$ is a boolean function that performs action a until all the conditions in c evaluate to $true$, in which case the function returns $true$; otherwise the function returns $false$ after t time-units have elapsed since the execution of the action a started.

- $getOnADAPT : S \times O \times R \rightarrow 2^{onCON} \times AD \times T$

  $getOnADAPT(s, o, r)$ returns a tuple (c, a, t) where c is the set of all ongoing conditions required for the subject s to keep the right r upon the object o during access, a is the adaptation action to be performed if any of the ongoing-conditions does not hold, and t is the time-out for this adaptation process.

- $getOnAltReq : S \times O \times R \rightarrow 2^{O \times R}$

  $getOnAltReq(s, o, r)$ denotes the set of alternative requests that can be made on behalf of the subject s when the initial request of the access right r upon the object o fails during access due to environmental conditions.

- $onD(s, o, r) = onAdapted(getOnADAPT(s, o, r))$

- $allowed(s, o, r) \Rightarrow true$

- The predicate $stopped$ is defined as follows:

$$stopped(s, o, r) \Rightarrow \left(\begin{array}{c} \neg onD(s, o, r) \\ \wedge \\ \bigwedge_{(o', r') \in F} stopped(s, o', r') \end{array} \right)$$

where $F = getOnAltReq(s, o, r)$ and '$V \Leftarrow W$' is equivalent to '$W \Rightarrow V$'.

3 Ubiquitous Learning System

3.1 Overview

A u-learning is a system that considers the context of learners, devices, services and environment in order to provide an appropriate and adaptable content, based on the current context. U-learning is based on an extremely large range of wireless, mobile, wearable, portable and embedded devices. Figure 1 below illustrates that u-learning infrastructural technology has two significant factors: devices that process the information, and the communication network. In addition, ubiquitous information processing is incorporated into office and home appliances as well as handheld and mobile devices; also, they are able to communicate with each other directly.

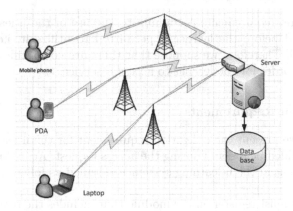

Fig. 1. U-learning system architecture

3.2 U-Learning Services

A u-learning system offers the following services based on the current context:

1. U-Lecture: this kind of service offers learners all possible lecture materials, which they can request and access through their mobile devices. There are three different types of u-lecture formats provided by the u-learning system: text, video and audio. In the u-learning system, each format requires a particular context in order for it to be delivered to the learner.

2. U-Test: this service is a formal approach for evaluating the learner's understanding of the u-learning content that has been requested and provided. It assesses the learner's knowledge and based on the results, the learners receive feedback to assist them in further u-learning. The learners utilize their mobile devices in accessing this service.

3. U-Tutorial: this type of service is used by learners to increase their knowledge in a particular subject; it is a useful service, as it provides an opportunity

for learners to obtain some form of self-assessment and to receive direct and personal feedback. This service is a combination of u-lecture and u-test. There are three different types of u-tutorial formats provided by the u-learning system: text, video and audio.

4   Requirements of the U-Learning System

A number of different requirements in the u-learning system must be fulfilled for the learner to gain access. The u-learning system requirements are: authorization requirements, obligation requirements, condition requirements and adaptation requirements.

4.1   Authorisation Requirements

The authorisation requirements pertaining to the use of the u-learning system must be satisfied before the learner is permitted to utilize it, i.e. the learner must be enrolled. Therefore, we suppose that there are no specific authorisation requirements in order for the learner to access a service.

4.2   Obligation Requirements

In this section we present the obligation requirement for the u-learning system; this must be fulfilled before and during the access request. Accordingly, the obligation requirement in the u-learning system is detailed as follows:

B1: The user must register on the module that includes the requested service before gaining access.

Condition Requirements. Condition requirements within the u-learning paradigm are defined as context requirements; these are considered by the system before and during the access request in order to permit access and delivery of the requested service to the learner. We present several condition requirements, as follows:

C1: The u-learning system considers the context of user in order to deliver the u-service. So, the only u-service format is allowed for a learner in *driving* context is the audio format.

C2: In the u-learning system at a university, the context of the learner is classified as private or public. The public context is defined as learners being in a location where making a noise is not permitted, such as in a library, seminar or lecture hall. On the other hand, the private context denotes that the learners are in a location where making a noise is permitted, such as in a cafe or at home. Therefore, the system provides u-services in any of the different formats (video, audio or text) but it considers the learner context before and during the access request. So, the only u-service format allowed for a learner in a public context is the text format. However, the system permits access to all the different u-service formats when the learner context is detected as private.

C3: As above, the u-learning system at a university provides u-services in different formats (video, audio and text); however, it considers the availability of the memory of the user's device before and during the access request. Each u-service format requires a different amount of space for memory space in order to facilitate access. If the learner requests a u-service in the video format, audio format or text format the available memory of the device (before the access request) must be more than 5MB, 2MB or 1MB respectively for access to be permitted. However, the available memory of the device (during the access request) must greater or equal to 1MB for all formats.

Adaptation Requirements. Adaptation requirements are defined as set of adaptation actions that are used by the system to adapt when conditions do not hold. In the u-learning system, there are several conditions, which have been explained in the previous section, and these conditions must be fulfilled before and during the access request. Otherwise, specific actions are performed by the system in order to adapt to a new situation. In addition, the system might issue an implicit request to access a specified alternative object, when there are no adaptation actions available or the adaptation action fails. Several adaptations are explained in the following paragraphs:

D1: If the context of the user is *driving* and the requested service is in video or text formats, the adaptation action is that the system issues an alternative request in order to deliver audio format instead.

D2: If the user requests the service in video or audio format when s/he is in a public place, the adaptation action is such that the system issues an alternative request that enables the user to access the service in text format instead.

D3: Again, if the user requests a u-service in video, audio or text formats, the required minimum available spaces in the memory (before the access) are 5MB, 2MB and 1MB, respectively and during the access is greater or equal to 1MB. The adaptation action in this case, if the conditions do not hold, is that the system activates garbage collector software in an attempt to make more space available in the memory.

Garbage Collector (GC) is a type of automatic memory management that attempts to dispose of objects or data that are no longer required, releasing the space that they had engaged.

5 Modelling U-Learning System in CA-UCON

In this section, we present the modelling of u-learning services in CA-UCON model. We adopt a finite set S of subjects and a finite set O of objects. The subjects are learners who are studying at a university and the objects are lecture, tutorial and test.

5.1   Right

These are the set of rights that the learners are allowed to invoke in accessing the u-learning services. For instance, the *downloading* right means that the learner is permitted to download a u-learning service (such as a u-lecture, u-tutorial or u-test) if all requirements pertaining to this right have been fulfilled.

$$R= \{download\}$$

Authorization. This is the authorization predicate, which checks the attributes of the subject and object in terms of the access right, both before the access and during the access. In this u-learning system, there are no authorization requirements for accessing the u-services. So, the authorization predicates are taken to be true. The authorization predicates are specified as follows:

– $PreA(ATT(s), ATT(o), r) = True.$
– $OnA(ATT(s), ATT(o), r) = True.$

5.2   Obligation

This is the obligation predicate, which must be fulfilled by the student before and during the access request. Obligation consists of three elements OBS, OBO and OB. The OBS is the set of subjects who perform the obligation action, while OBO is the set of objects on which the obligation is to be performed. The OB is the set of obligation actions that the subject must perform in order to access the object. Therefore, the obligation is specified as follows:

– $OBS = S.$
– $OBO = O.$
– $OB = \{register\}.$
  The obligation action as shown above is *register*, which means that the learner (who would like to request a service by invoking a right) must register with the requested service.

– $getPreOBL(s, o, r) = \{(s, o, register)\}.$

  This function means that for each user who would like to access any service by using any right, s/he has to register to the module which includes the requested service.
– $allowed(s, o, r) \Rightarrow PreFulfilled(getPreOBL(s, o, r)).$

Condition. This is the condition predicate, which checks the condition of access request before and during the access. We use a variable *StudentContext* to denote the context of learner; its possible values are: *driving*, when the context of the learner is *driving*; *public*, when the context of the learner is in a *public* place and *private*, when the context of the learner is in *private* place. Accordingly, the conditions are specified as follows:

C1: The user should not be driving when requesting a u-video or u-text service. This is specified by the condition:

$$(StudentContext \neq driving) \tag{1}$$

C2: In a public place, the user may not access a u-video or u-audio service; s/he may only access a u-text service. This is specified by the condition:

$$(StudentContext = Private) \tag{2}$$

C3: The user must have sufficient memory available on her/his mobile device, which must be more than 5MB if s/he requests the service in video format, more than 2MB if in audio, and more than 1MB if the requested service is in text format before the access request. However, during the access the memory available must greater or equal to 1MB for all formats. We use the variable *AvailableMemory* to denote the amount of free space available in the memory. This is specified by the conditions:

$$(AvailableMemory > 5MB) \tag{3}$$

$$(AvailableMemory > 2MB) \tag{4}$$

$$(AvailableMemory > 1MB) \tag{5}$$

$$(AvailableMemory >= 1MB) \tag{6}$$

PreCon= OnCon={Eq.(1),Eq.(2), Eq.(3),Eq.(4),Eq.(5),Eq.(6)}

5.3   Adaptation

Adaptation requirements are a set of adaptation actions that are used by the system to adapt when specific conditions do not hold. In particular, there are four adaptation actions: *AdaptToVideo*, *AdaptToAudio*, *AdaptToText* and *skip*. We use the variable *gc* to model the garbage collector; this variable can only have two values: 1 (to mean that the garbage collector is activated) or 0 (to deactivate it). The action *skip* means that the action is not initiated; it lasts for only one time-unit. The adaptation actions are specified as follows:

AD= {*AdaptToVideo, AdaptToAudio, AdaptToText, Skip*}.

In the u-learning system, the service (O) is specified by this set:

$$O = O_{video} \bigcup O_{audio} \bigcup O_{text}.$$

which means that O_{video} is a video version of u-lecture, u-tutorial and u-test, O_{audio} is an audio version of u-lecture, u-tutorial and u-test, and O_{text} is a text version of u-lecture, u-tutorial and u-test.

getPreADAPT=getOnADAPT(s,o,download)= ({(Eq.(1),Eq.(2), Eq.(3), (Eq.(6)) }, AdaptToVideo, 5)
for $o \in O_{video}$

This function means that if the user requests the video format and if one (or all) of these conditions does not hold, the system will adapt by performing a number of different actions through the function *AdaptToVideo*; this includes all possible actions in an attempt to make the condition true. We suppose that the time taken for the adaptation actions in *AdaptToVideo* to be performed in this system is *5 seconds*.

The action *AdaptToVideo* is defined as follows:

AdaptToVideo = $(if \neg(Eq.(1))$ *then*   *Skip*
|| $if \neg(Eq.(2))$ *then*   *Skip*
|| $if \neg(Eq.(3))$ *then* $gc := 1$
|| $if \neg(Eq.(6))$ *then* $gc := 1$
)

This function includes all possible actions that the system employs in adapting to a new situation if the conditions do not hold when the user requests a u-service in the video format.

getPreADAPT=getOnADAPT(s,o,download)= ({Eq.(2), Eq.(4), (Eq.(6)) }, AdaptToAudio, 4)
for $o \in O_{audio}$

This function means that if the user requests the audio format and if one (or all) of these conditions does not hold, the system will adapt by performing a number of different actions through the function *AdaptToAudio*; this includes all possible actions in an attempt to make the condition true. We suppose that the time taken for the adaptation actions in *AdaptToAudio* to be performed in this system is *4 seconds*.

The action *AdaptToAudio* is defined as follows :

AdaptToAudio = $(if \neg(Eq.(2))$ *then*   *Skip*
|| $if \neg(Eq.(4))$ *then* $gc := 1$
|| $if \neg(Eq.(6))$ *then* $gc := 1$
)

This function includes all possible actions that the system employs in adapting to a new situation if the conditions do not hold when the user requests a u-service in the audio format.

getPreADAPT=getOnADAPT(s,o,download)= ({Eq.(1), Eq.(5), (Eq.(6)) }, AdaptToText, 3)
for $o \in O_{text}$

This function means that if the user requests the text format and if one (or all) of these conditions does not hold, the system will adapt by performing a number of different actions through the function $AdaptToText$; this includes all possible actions in an attempt to make the condition true. We suppose that the time taken for the adaptation actions in $AdaptToText$ to be performed in this system is *3 seconds*.

The action $AdaptToText$ is defined as follows:

AdaptToText $= (if\neg(Eq.(1))$ *then*   *Skip*
$\|$ $if\neg(Eq.(5))$ *then* $gc := 1$
$\|$ $if\neg(Eq.(6))$ *then* $gc := 1$
$)$

This function includes all possible actions that the system employs in adapting to a new situation if the conditions do not hold when the user requests a u-service in the text format.

In the following section , we consider the following functions :

$Video : O \longrightarrow O_{video}$ video(o)= the video version of object(o).
$Audio : O \longrightarrow O_{audio}$ audio(o)= the audio version of object(o).
$Text : O \longrightarrow O_{text}$ text(o)= the text version of object(o).

$$getPreAltReq = getOnAltReq(s, o, download) = \\ \{(Audio(o), download)\} \tag{7}$$

for $o \in O_{video}$

$$getPreAltReq = getOnAltReq(s, o, download) = \\ \{(Audio(o), download)\} \tag{8}$$

for $o \in O_{text}$

In the functions above, if the user requests a u-service the video or text format when driving, in this case the condition does not hold; the system then issues an alternative request, which delivers that u-service in the audio format instead.

$$getPreAltReq = getOnAltReq(s, o, download) = \\ \{(Text(o), download)\} \tag{9}$$

for $o \in O_{video}$

$$getPreAltReq = getOnAltReq(s, o, download) = \\ \{(Text(o), download)\} \tag{10}$$

for $o \in O_{audio}$

The functions above mean that if the user requests a u-service in the video or audio format when in a public place, the system then issues an alternative request, which delivers that u-service in the text format instead.

6   Validation

In this section, we present the validation of our CA-UCON model vis-a-vis the above u-learning system. We illustrate how u-learning system properties can be validated using the execution environment of *CCA* [3]. We then devise scenarios and execute them in order to validate two main classes of system properties as proposed by [2]:

> *Safety property: stating that nothing bad will happen.*
> *Liveness property: stating that something good will happen,*
> *eventually*

Scenario 1: the property to validate in this scenario is : " *if the pre-authorization or the pre-obligation requirement is not met before the access then, the access request will be denied by the system*". Suppose a learner requests to download a u-lecture in the video format and the context of learner is in *private* place and the memory capacity of her/his mobile device is more than 5MB. However, the pre-authorization requirements of this access request are not met. In this case, the system has to deny the access request.

```
*************************************************
    **                                   **
    **                                   **
    **       CCA Interpreter version 4.01    **
    **             October 2012              **
    **                                   **
    **      Please send error messages to    **
    **          - fsiewe@dmu.ac.uk           **
    **          - fsiewe@yahoo.fr            **
    **                                   **
    **                                   **
*************************************************

CCA Parser Version 4.01: Reading from file ca_ucon6.cca . . .
CCA Parser Version 4.01: CCA program parsed successfully.

Execution mode: interleaving

1--->  (local call to the abstraction "mem" in the ambient "root")
2--->  (Sibling to sibling: subject ===(P1,video,download)===> requesting)
3--->  (Sibling to sibling: requesting ===(P1,video,download)===> checkpreA)
4--->  (Sibling to sibling: checkpreA ===(0)===> requesting)
5--->  (Sibling to sibling: requesting ===(denyA,video,download)===> subject)

Done
```

Fig. 2. Execution of Scenario 1

Figure 2 illustrates the execution of scenario 1. The subject sends the access request containing the subject ID, the u-lecture in the video format and the downloading right to the *requesting* ambient (line 2). The *requesting* ambient receives the access request and checks the *pre-authorisation* pertaining to this request (line 3). So, the *pre-authorization* of this request is not met, and finally the system denied the access request (lines 4-5).

Scenario 2: The property to validate in this scenario is : " *if the pre-authorization, pre-obligation and pre-condition requirements are met at the time of access request and on-authorization, on-obligation and on-condition requirements continuously hold during the access, the access will end successfully*". Suppose a learner requests to download a u-lecture in the video format and the context of learner is in *private* place and the memory capacity of her/his mobile device is more than 5MB. The service will be delivered to the learner by the system.

```
           **                         **
           **                         **
       *********************************************
       CCA Parser Version 4.01:  Reading from file ca_ucon6.cca . . .
       CCA Parser Version 4.01:  CCA program parsed successfully.
       Execution mode: interleaving
       1 --->   (Sibling to sibling: subject === (P1,video,download) ===> requesting)
       2 --->   (Sibling to sibling: requesting === (P1,video,download) ===> checkpreA)
       3 --->   (Sibling to sibling: requesting === (1) ===> requesting)
       4 --->   (Sibling to sibling: requesting === (P1,video,download) ===> checkpreB)
       5 --->   (Sibling to sibling: checkpreB === (P1) ===> UP)
       6 --->   (Sibling to sibling: UP === (1) ===> checkpreB)
       7 --->   (Sibling to sibling: checkpreB === (1) ===> requesting)
       8 --->   (Sibling to sibling: requesting === (P1,video,download) ===> checkpreC)
       9 --->   (Child to parent: checkpreC === (P1,context) ===> SubjectCxt)
       10--->   (Child to parent: SubjectCxt === (P1,private) ===> checkpreC)
       11--->   (Child to parent: checkpreC === (P1,fm) ===> MemorySize)
       12--->   (Child to parent: MemorySize === (P1,6) ===> checkpreC)
       13--->   (Child to parent: checkpreC === (P1,bandwidth) ===> Bandwidth)
       14--->   (Child to parent: Bandwidth === (P1,high) ===> checkpreC)
       15--->   (Sibling to sibling: checkpreC === (1) ===> requesting)
       16--->   (Sibling to sibling: requesting === (PERMIT,video,download) ===> subject)
       17--->   (Sibling to sibling: requesting === (P1,video,download) ===> preUpdate)
       18--->   (Sibling to sibling: preUpdate === (5) ===> francois_credit)
       19--->   (Sibling to sibling: francois_credit === () ===> preUpdate)
       20--->   (Sibling to sibling: preUpdate === (done) ===> requesting)
       21--->   (Sibling to sibling: requesting === (P1,video,download) ===> accessing)
       22--->   (Sibling to sibling: accessing === (P1,video,download) ===> checkonA)
       23--->   (Sibling to sibling: checkonA === (1) ===> accessing)
       24--->   (Sibling to sibling: accessing === (P1,video,download) ===> checkonB)
       25--->   (Sibling to sibling: checkonB === (1) ===> accessing)
       26--->   (Sibling to sibling: accessing === (P1,video,download) ===> checkonC)
       27--->   (Sibling to sibling: checkonC === (1) ===> accessing)
       28--->   (Sibling to sibling: accessing === (P1,video,download) ===> onUpdate)
       29--->   (Sibling to sibling: onUpdate === (1) ===> francois_credit)
       30--->   (Local: francois_credit === (5) ===> francois_credit)
       31--->   (Sibling to sibling: francois_credit === () ===> onUpdate)
       32--->   (Sibling to sibling: onUpdate === (done) ===> accessing)
       33--->   (Sibling to sibling: subject === (END_USAGE,video,download) ===> accessing)
       34--->   (Sibling to sibling: accessing === (P1,video,download) ===> postUpdate)
       35--->   (Sibling to sibling: postUpdate === (0) ===> francois_credit)
       36--->   (Sibling to sibling: francois_credit === () ===> postUpdate)
       37--->   (Sibling to sibling: postUpdate === (done) ===> accessing)
       38--->   (Sibling to sibling: accessing === (ENDED_SUCCESSFULLY,video,download) ===> subject)
       done
```

Fig. 3. Execution of Scenario2

Figure 3 presents a screen shot of the execution of Scenario 2, from which it can be seen that the subject sends the access request to the *requesting* ambient (line 2). The *requesting* ambient receives the access request and checks the *pre-authorisation, pre-obligation* and *pre-conditions* pertaining to this request (lines 3-8). The ambient *checkPreC* checks the context of the subject, the memory capacity of the mobile device and the bandwidth of the network before access. In this case, all the requirements before the access are met and the access is *permit* to the service(lines 16). Moreover, the *requesting* ambient sends the access request to *accessing* ambient to check *on-authorisation, on-obligation* and *on-conditions* pertaining to this request, and all requirements are hold during the access (lines 22-27). In line(33) The subject ended the access successfully by sending this message END_USAGE to the *accessing* ambient.

7   Related Work

U-learning is system considers the context of learner, services and environment in order to deliver the service in adaptive way. The major concern of accepting and using such system is security issue,so the need for an adaptive usage control to control the services in ubiquitous environment is significant. Some recent works have been done to improve the UCON model in order to overcome the short-coming of UCON in ubiquitous environment. For instance, [9] proposed a new access control model called TUCON (Times-based Usage Control) for prevention of digital resources abuse. In TUCON a time variable is introduced into UCON, and maximum times defined as consumption constraints. This approach is eas-ily defined in CA-UCON model by specified the time as condition requirement. [10] proposed Geography Usage Control (GEO-UCON) model to deal with GEO DBMS access control. In GEO-UCON a geospatial factor is added into UCON to ensure data security in location-based services and mobile applications. This model like the last one, can be defined in CA-UCON model where the location can be used as condition requirement to control the service. Moreover, [11] ex-tends usage control model to context-aware in mobile computing environments. They introduced two new components into UCON model: context and states. The new model called ConUCON takes these new components plus obligations on access decisions. [12] proposed a new model called CUC model which replaces the conditions component in UCON by context and add a management module to it. The last two models are using the context only to control the resources by changing the condition component into context, which is basically the UCON model can do that. None of these models is model and validate usage control in ubiquitous learning system. UCON model has condition component which can sense the environment context, but it cannot adapt to the new situation based on this context. Unlike the above UCON extensions, CA-UCON model enables adaptation to environmental changes in the aim of preserving continuity of ac-cess by triggering specific actions to adapt to new situations. In addition to data protection, CA-UCON model enhances the quality of services, striving to keep explicit interactions with the user at a minimum. This makes it more suitable for pervasive computing systems.

8   Conclusion and Future Work

In this paper, we have demonstrated modelling of usage control in a u-learning system using CA-UCON . We illustrate how u-learning system properties can be validated using the execution environment of *CCA*. We proposed some scenarios and run them in order to check the usage control of u-learning system using CA-UCON in varying context.

In future works, we will investigate possible enforcement mechanisms of the CA-UCON model in a pervasive environment.

References

1. Almutairi, A., Siewe, F.: CA-UCON: A Context-Aware Usage Control Model. In: Proceeding of the 5th ACM International Workshop on Context-Awareness for Self-Managing Systems (CASEMANS 2011), pp. 34–38 (2011)
2. Owicki, S., Lamport, L.: Proving liveness properties of concurrent programs. ACM Trans. Program. Lang. Syst. 4(3), 455–495 (1982)
3. Siewe, F., Zedan, H., Cau, A.: The Calculus of Context-aware Ambients. Journal of Computer and System Sciences 77(4), 597–620 (2011)
4. Jaehong, P., Ravi, S.: The UCON: Usage Control Model. Journal of ACM Transactions on Information and System Security 7(1), 128–174 (2004)
5. Horvath, I., Peck, D.: Survey of Advanced Learning Solutions from Methodological and technological perspectives. In: Proceedings of 24th ASCILITE Conference, Singapore (2009)
6. Almutairi, S., Aldabbas, H., Abu-Samaha, A.: Review on the security related issues in context aware system. International Journal of Wireless & Mobile Networks (IJWMN) 4(3), 195–204 (2012)
7. Cardelli, L., Gordon, A.: Mobile ambients. Theoretical Computer Science 240, 177–213 (2000)
8. Sangiorgi, D., Walker, D.: PI-Calculus: A Theory of Mobile Processes. Cambridge University Press, New York (2001)
9. Zhao, B., Sandhu, R., Zhang, X., Qin, X.: Towards a Times-Based Usage Control Model. In: Barker, S., Ahn, G.-J. (eds.) Data and Applications Security 2007. LNCS, vol. 4602, pp. 227–242. Springer, Heidelberg (2007)
10. Hong-jun, H.: Study and application of special access control model based on UCON. Master Thesis. Nanjing: Jiangshu University (2009)
11. Bai, G., Gu, L., Feng, T., Guo, Y., Chen, X.: Context-Aware Usage Control for Android. In: Jajodia, S., Zhou, J. (eds.) SecureComm 2010. LNICST, vol. 50, pp. 326–343. Springer, Heidelberg (2010)
12. Xiaoofeng, L., Ling, L., Ail, L., Wanbo, L.: The Contextual Usage Control Model. Journal of Zhejiang University Science C (Computers & Electronics) ZUSC-D-12-00217 (2012)
13. Graschew, G., Roelofs, T., Rakowsky, A., Schalg, S.: From e-learning towards ulearning: ICT enabled ubiquitous learning and training (200x)

An Approach for Context-Aware Service Selection Using QoS and User Preferences

Mohcine Madkour[1], Mohamed Bakhouya[2], Abdelilah Maach[1], and Driss El Ghanami[1]

[1] Ecole Mohammadia d'Ingenieurs, Mohamed V-Agdal University, Rabat, Morocco
mouhcine.madkour@gmail.com, {maach,elghanami}@emi.ac.ma
[2] Aalto University, Otakaari 4, 00076, Aalto, Finland
mohamed.bakhouya@aalto.fi

Abstract. Ubiquitous computing refers to building a global computing environment where seamless and invisible access to computing resources is provided to users. The successful application of pervasive services relies on its ability to provide efficient and cost-effective QoS (Quality of Service) support. This paper introduces a service selection approach based on QoS and user preferences. Simulations have been conducted and preliminary results are reported to show the usefulness and the importance of using QoS and user preferences in service selection process.

Keywords: Ubiquitous and pervasive computing, Context-aware service selection, service adaptation, QoS-aware, user preferences and service policies.

1 Introduction

Ubiquitous computing has revolutionized the way humans interact with the world around them. The widespread use of wearable devices and the seamless connectivity between them have transcended the traditional computing era to the pervasive computing era. The later enables new opportunities for a user to perform his/her operations everywhere and anytime [16,17,5]. Each user has different expectations for a particular service, which requires a context-aware and user-centric selection process. However, the process has to overcome challenges exposed by uncertainty and fuzziness of context information. These challenges make it difficult to select a service that provide the appropriate QoS and meet user preferences. Current approaches for service selection are typically based on exact matches between offered and requested service capabilities. These approaches are inefficient when the context is fuzzy or uncertain [3,4].

In ubiquitous and pervasive environments, a service usually possesses a set of QoS parameters, though many of them are of dynamic nature, i.e., related to the service execution environment, a service can still advertise its assumed QoS [6,7]. QoS policies are rules related to QoS parameters, such as bandwidth and response time. QoS policy of services includes both functional and non-functional properties. Functional properties can be measured in terms of throughput, latency, response time, whereas

M. Matera and G. Rossi (Eds.): MobiWIS 2013 Workshops, CCIS 183, pp. 110–119, 2013.
© Springer International Publishing Switzerland 2013

non-functional properties contain non quantifiable metrics, such as integrity, reliability, availability, and security [1]. Therefore, QoS parameters should be taken into account by the service selection process. Furthermore, user preferences are underlying criteria that are required to make the service adaptable and useful.

The contribution of this paper is twofold: First, we focus on non-functional and QoS aspects in service description to select a set of services according to their appropriateness to quality attributes of user context. Second, we define a policy-based adaptation scheme as the automatic selection of the best policy for delivering the service to user. The remainder of this paper is organized as follows. Section 2 presents briefly related work. Section 3 introduces the selection process and describes the policy-based and QoS-aware adaptation scheme. Section 4 presents the preliminary simulation results. Conclusions and future work are given in Section 5.

2   Related Work

Service descriptions are used to advertise the service capabilities, interface, behavior, and quality. Publication of such information about available services provides the necessary means for discovery and selection of services [17]. In particular, the QoS description [2] provides functional and non-functional service quality attributes, such as service metering and cost, performance metrics (e.g., response time), security attributes, integrity, reliability, scalability, and availability. Moreover, quality of service plays an important role in automatic service selection. It is mainly used to establish valid and reliable service and identify the best offers from a set of functionally similar ones.

Recent studies emphasized that selection process can be viewed as graph matching problem. More precisely, with the development of service-oriented computing environments, QoS-aware service selection has been a more and more important research issue. In service selection, QoS evaluation in matching process are always aggregated for computing the QoS of matches, which has been reported in many previous studies. The work [14] and [15] emphasized the definition of QoS aspects and metrics. In [12], a model for web service discovery with QoS constraints, called WSDM-Q, is proposed. A set of QoS categorization *tModel* and a kind of reputation categorization *tModel* are defined in the model to describe the QoS attributes of a service and the degree of guaranteed QoS delivered by a service respectively. The concept of quantification is introduced in the model to transform between the QoS attributes and QoS categorizations. In [13], a QoS-Guaranteed and distributed mechanism of Web service discovery is proposed. It supports Web service discovery with QoS constraints and enhances the QoS of service discovery system.

However, the above approaches have several limitations. For example, there are situations that some QoS attributes cannot be matched exactly with user query due to the fuzziness of context. In other words, it is difficult to get from user query the same expressions as in service description, e.g., a user wants a hotel that is five min far away from the city center, while in service description we acquire the hotel is 15 km from city center, or a user requests maximum reliability, whereas in the description the reliability is set to be 75%. Furthermore, QoS values always vary based on different contexts for different types of service invocation. When multiple preferences exist over the QoS attributes of services, it is always difficult to maximize all the QoS attributes because there might always be anti-correlated relations between them.

3   Selection and Adaptation Process

3.1   Service Selection

A process model can be represented as a workflow graph, where the vertices represent "activities" and the edges represent the precedencies between "activities". Fig. 1-a and Fig.1-b show an example of workflows for user's query and service respectively. They are represented as graphs annotated with semantic QoS attributes, similar to the approach proposed in [8].

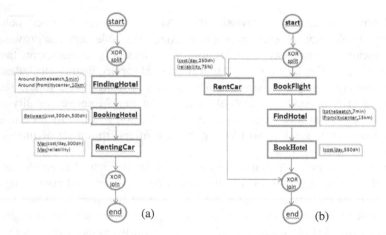

Fig. 1. a) Request workflow graph, b) Service workflow graph

In order to select the best suitable service for a given query two similarity functions are used, *structural similarity* and *semantic similarity*. For computing structural similarity, we consider that a process is represented by a graph $G=(N,E)$, where N is the nodes and E is the edges. Given two graphs, a similarity score can be obtained by computing their *graph-edit distance* as described in [9]. The *graph-edit distance* between two graphs is the minimal number of graph-edit operations that is required to get from one graph to another. This operation can be seen as a mapping process between two graphs. For example, let us consider $G_1=(N_1,E_1)$ and $G_2=(N_2,E_2)$ are two workflow graphs of process models. The mapping between G_1 and G_2 is defined as the partial injective mapping $M:(N_1{\rightarrow}N_2)U(E_1{\rightarrow}E_2)$ that maps nodes and edges. Indeed, to go from G_1 to G_2, three operations are possible: *i)* inserting nodes or edges, *ii)* deleting nodes or edges, and *iii)* substituting nodes or edges (the alteration of the label of node or edge).We assume that *ID* (Inserted or Deleted) is the set of all inserted and deleted nodes or edges and *SB* (SuBstituted) is the set of all substituted nodes or edges. The mapping distance is defined as $D = |ID| + |SB| + \sum_{n,m \in M} 1 - SynSym(n,m)$, where *SynSym* is the syntactic similarity [22]. The *graph-edit distance* similarity, denoted by *Str-Sim*, is then computed as one minus the average of the following values: the fraction of cardinal of inserted or deleted nodes, the fraction of cardinal of inserted or deleted edges, and the average distance of substituted nodes [22]:

$$Str\text{-}Sim = 1 - \left\{ \frac{|ID|}{|N_1| + |N_2|}, \frac{|SB|}{|E_1| + |E_2|}, \frac{2 \cdot \sum_{n,m \in M} 1 - SynSym(n,m)}{|N_1| + |N_2| - |ID|} \right\}$$

Instead of using a plain average of the three components, we can use a weighted average. It's worth noting that each service query process supports a set of QoS requirements according to the current context, such as throughput, reliability, response time, and cost. These QoS attributes are always attached to its semantic values. Usually the majority of QoS attributes of a given context are not exactly value-fixed in service request. Therefore, for evaluating the QoS attributes of a given context in a query process, we consider the membership functions that represent the predicates interpreting the quality attributes. For example, as illustrated in Fig. 1, where each pair $(r_i; a_j)$ is linked with a membership function, r_i is a request attribute of node i and a_j is its corresponding annotation in applicant service a. An example is provided in Table 1. The work presented in this paper considers that a mapping algorithm is already given, such as the one presented in [10] in order to map two process models.

Table 1. QoS semantic similarity elements

Request attribute	Serive annotation	QoS Semantic evaluation
r_{m_1}: *around* (tothebeatch,5min)	a_{m_1}: (tothebeatch, 7min)	$QSem - Eval(r_{m_1}, r_{m_1})$
r_{m_2}: *around* (fromcitycenter,10km)	a_{m_2}: (fromcitycenter, 15km)	$QSem - Eval(r_{m_2}, r_{m_2})$
r_{m_3}: *between*(cost,300dh,500dhs)	a_{m_3}: (cost/day,550dh)	$QSem - Eval(r_{m_3}, r_{m_3})$
r_{m_4}: *max*(cost/day,300dh)	a_{m_4}: (cost/day,250dh)	$QSem - Eval(r_{m_4}, r_{m_4})$
r_{m_5}: *max*(reliability)	a_{m_5}: (reliability, 75%)	$QSem - Eval(r_{m_5}, r_{m_5})$

After mapping the two graphs, a list of nodes that match each other is obtained. Then, the semantic similarity can be computed from atomic pairs $(r_i; a_j)$. To do so, we consider the membership function of each semantic QoS expression in order to compute the truth degree of each expression r_i as shown in Table 2.

Table 2. QoS semantic similarity computing between matched pairs

Request attribute	r_{m_1}	r_{m_2}	r_{m_3}	r_{m_4}	r_{m_5}
Membership function of the request attribute	μ_{m_1} [ToTheBeatch]	μ_{m_2} [FromCity Center]	μ_{m_3} [cost]	μ_{m_4} [cost,300]	μ_{m_5} [reliability]
Evaluation	0,65	0,5	0,9	1	0,85

We aggregate the semantic similarity values by using the linguistic quantifier "*almost all*"[11]. More precisely, the natural interpretation of the similarities between a request r and an applicant a process model is "Almost all semantic preferences of r are satisfied by a". For example, using values provided in Fig. 1, the overall semantic QoS similarity can be computed as follows: $QSem - Eval(r_{m_4}, a_{m_4}) = 1 \geq QSem - Eval(r_{m_5}, a_{m_5}) = 0,9 \geq QSem - Eval(r_{m_3}, a_{m_3}) = 0,85 \geq QSem - Eval(r_{m_1}, a_{m_1}) = 0,65 \geq QSem - Eval(r_{m_2}, a_{m_2}) = 0$. Therefore, the overall similarity degree can be obtained by computing the following expression $max(min(1, \mu_Q\left(\frac{1}{5}\right), min(0,9, \mu_Q\left(\frac{2}{5}\right), min(0,85, \mu_Q\left(\frac{3}{5}\right), min(0,65, \mu_Q\left(\frac{4}{5}\right), min(0,5, \mu_Q\left(\frac{5}{5}\right))$. The value obtained is 0.65, which means that 65% of nodes are semantically similar. This is expected since there are three nodes among five that have a similarity degree greater than 0.65.

It should be noted that using these functions, several services could match the user request. In order to select the best suitable one, two ranking methods could be used. In the first method, the average value of both structural and semantic degrees (either with weighing them or without) is used. Thus the resulting degree handles both criteria, and the ranking is based on this overall degree. In the second method, the success rate for the structural degree is considered. If it reaches some degree, which is an acceptable matching, then we rank-order by only the semantic degree satisfaction, otherwise, the matching is not reachable and thus the process model is ignored. This service selection mechanism addresses the quality attributes in service description to enable the fully-automatic selection of services. It supports semantic QoS service description and matchmaking, works system-wide, and could yield to a good retrieval rate.

3.2 Policy-Based Adaptation

The adaptation approach taking into consideration service policies is described as follows. The first M services are first taken from the output of the context-aware service selection process described in Section 3.1. The number M depends on user preferences and service features to let for more flexibility in service selection and adaptation schemes. Indeed, the policies of the M selected services are considered in the adaptation process. This process is a fuzzy-based adaptation using fitness functions. More precisely, let us consider $S = \{S_1, S_2, ..., S_M\}$ a set of selected services, where $S_i, (1 \leq i \leq M)$ represents the i-th service, and M is the number of services. In the rest of this section, some definitions and terminologies are first given and adapted from the work presented in [18].

- **Policy:** represents a mode used to deliver a service with a certain resource requirement and a quality-of-service condition. Let's consider $P_i = \{p_i^1, p_i^2, ..., p_i^{m_i}\}, i \in [1, M]$ a set of policies, which can be adopted for delivering the $i - th$ service, where m_i is the number of the policies of service S_i.
- **Preference Context:** Let's consider $C = \{c_1, c_2, ..., c_n\}$ a set of context attributes used to build preferences in order to monitor all services S_i, where c_i represents the i-th context information and n is the number of monitored contexts.
- **Preference Situation:** A preference situation (PS) is a combination of preferences. Let's consider $LV = \{Lv_1, Lv_2, ..., Lv_k)$ a set of linguistic values. The preference situation at time t, denoted by $PS(t)$, can be represented by a set of 3-element tuples: $PS(t) = \{(c_a, Lv_b, \mu_{c_a Lv_b}(prefered - value(c_a, t))\}$, where $(prefered - value(c_a, t))$ represents the suitable value of context c_a at time t; and $\mu_{c_a Lv_b}(x)$ is the predefined membership function of c_a is Lv_b".

It is worth noting that each policy p_i^j of $S_i \in S$ is associated with a most suitable preference situation (PS). Therefore, the Standard Reference of p_i^j can be computed as follows: $SR(p_i^j) = \{(c_a, Lv_b, \mu_{c_a Lv_b}(Most - Suited - value(c_a, t))$. $SRD(P_i)$ is the Standard Reference Depository, which represents the aggregation $\{SR(p_i^1), SR(p_i^2), \dots SR(p_i^{m_i})\}$. Therefore, the fuzzy adaptation process can be defined as a mapping process from the set of preferences situation PS to a set of all candidates' policies $P_{candidates}$. It aims to find the most suitable policies from $P_{candidates}$ by making the tradeoff between QoS and user preferences. So, the adaptation process computes the appropriate fitness function of all elements in $P_{candidates}$ in order to select the most suitable policy. We propose to use reciprocals of Manhattan [20], Minkowsky [19] and Chebychev [21] distances as fitness functions:

$$FF - Manhattan(p_i^j) = \frac{1}{\sum_{k=1}^{sizeof(SR(p_i^j))} |\mu(Most - suited - value(c_k, t)) - \mu(prefered - value(c_k, t))|}$$

$$FF - Minkowsky\,(p_i^j) = \frac{1}{\sum_{k=1}^{sizeof(SR(p_i^j))} |(\mu(Most - suited - value(c_k, t)) - \mu(prefered - value(c_k, t))|^{p_k})^{1/r_k}}$$

$$FF - Chebychev(p_i^j) = \frac{1}{max_{k=1}^{sizeof(SR(p_i^j))} (|\mu(Most - suited - value(c_k, t)) - \mu(prefered - value(c_k, t))|)}$$

Where $sizeof(SR(p_i^j))$ represents the number of tuples in $SR(p_i^j)$, $\mu(x)$ is the membership function predefined for i-th vector, and we consider two set of integers $p = \{p_k, k\ is\ integer\}$ and $r\{r_k, k\ is\ integer\}$. It is worth noting that in Minowky-based fitness function we independently configure the two set of powers p and r to find the balance between the large number of different elements and the importance of the difference between two terms.

The concept of fitness function is inspired by the membership function in classical fuzzy logic theory. But the two are different, i.e., the value of fitness degree is a positive number but not limited into [0,1], and the sum of fitness degree for all the policies of a service is not equal to 1. The value of fitness degree only indicates to which degree a policy is suitable for the current environment. In the above three functions, the divisors are for the calculation of the distance between PS and $SR(p_i^j)$. After obtaining the *crisp distance*, we compute its inverse to get the fitness degree. For instance, if the distance between PS and $SR(p_i^j)$ is 0, which means that current Preference Situation and $SR(p_i^j)$ have a perfect match, then the fitness degree is infinite. In general, the fitness degree decreases with the increase of the distance and vice versa.

4   Simulation Results

In order to evaluate the selection and adaptation process, we have used the following scenario. Let us consider that Otman is situated in a University campus and uses a PDA devise, which is equipped by a context-aware Campus Assistant application. Otman can then exchange emails and messages with his colleagues inside the campus. Let's assume that the application runs *chat* and *email* services. Otman uses the PDA to send and receive emails through the university's email server, and to chat with colleagues as well. The services provided by the Campus Assistant application have alternative policies according to real-time context. For example, in order to distribute messages among chatting participants, Campus Assistant service helps in making a suitable choice among three policies: *textChat* to deliver text messages; *voiceChat* to exchange voice messages; and *videoChat* to exchange video messages. The email service operates in a similar fashion. Students can check their emails using one of the following five policies: *head-Mail*: which delivers only the mail header and a notice signifying that the transmitting operation is not over and will continue when an elevated network bandwidth and other circumstances are available; *fullMail*: which conveys mail in full-text; *encryptedMail*: which sends encrypted email; *bigMail*: which conveys email in full-text and attachments; and *encryptedBigMail*, which conveys encrypted big-emails.

We assume that the output of the selection process and their corresponding policies are: S = {chat, email}; P_1 ={textChat(p_1^1), voiceChat(p_1^2), videoChat(p_1^3)}; P_2 ={headMail (p_2^1) ,fullMail (p_2^2) ,encryptedMail (p_2^3) ,bigMail (p_2^4) , Mail (p_2^5)}. We consider the following context types over which the users have preferences:

C={Network_bandwidth(c_1),Processor_clockRate(c_2),Response_delay(c_3),Memory_freeSpace$(c_{4)}$}; and we concider the linguistic terms: LV = {high, low}.

So, PS(current-time)={

(**Network − maxRate**, high, $\mu_{Network-maxRate,high}$ $(prefered − value(network − maxRate, t)))$,

(**CPU − ClockRate**, high, $\mu_{CPU-ClockRate,high}$ $(prefered − value(CPU − ClockRate, t)))$,

(**Network − Delay**, low, $\mu_{Network-Delay,Low}$ $(prefered − value(Network − Delay, t))$,

(**RAM − freeSpace**, high, $\mu_{RAM-freeSpace,High}$ $(prefered − value(RAM − freeSpace, t))))$}

The membership function of the used linguistic terms is represented in Fig. 2. We have also other preferences such as User Privacy Intervention (UPI), if a user want to protect its privacy then $P_1' = \{p_1^1, p_1^2\}$ and $P_2' = \{p_2^1, p_2^3, p_2^5\}$, else $P_1' = P_1$ and $P_2' = P_2$, and energy saving, if the energy level of the battery is less than 5%, then$P_1' = P_1$ and$P_2' = \{p_2^1\}$. The suitable context values for all policies of P_1 and P_2 , considered in the evaluations, are shown in Table 3.

Table 3. Most suitable context values for policies

	c_1 (kbps)	c_2 (MHz)	c_3 (ms)	c_4 (MB)
p_1^1	4	20	500	0,2
p_1^2	200	300	10	4
p_1^3	10000	1000	0,2	200
p_2^1	2	4	---	0,2
p_2^2	10	10	---	0,4
p_2^3	10	100	----	10
p_2^4	500	50	---	2
p_2^5	500	1000	---	100

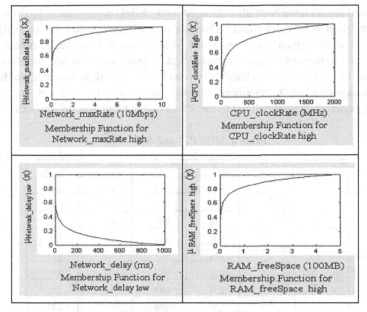

Fig. 2. Predefined membership functions

Network_bandwidth=10kps	Processor_clockRate= 10 MHZ	Response_delay=100ms
Memory_freeSpace= 10 MB	I_{UPI} =0	Energy_Level= 40%

Fig. 3. Current QoS information

After computing the preference situation, the service adaptation process can be performed. The following steps are then used to compute SRD using the values shown in Fig. 3:

- Use the fuzzy sets to interpret current preference situation: PS(current) = {(Network_maxRate, high, 0.20), (Processor_clockRate, high, 0.23), (Nework_delay, low, 0.25), (Memory_freeSpace, high, 0.58)}.
- Use privacy preferences and battery energy to filter P_1 and P_2, and get $P_1' = P_1$ and $P_2' = P_2$
- Use the membership functions depicted in Fig. 2 to calculate SRD(P_1') and SRD(P_2'). Results obtained are shown in Table 4.
- We simulate the three fitness functions. For the Minkowsky fitness function, we consider that all *r values are* equals to 1 and *p* takes 2 for chat service, for email service we consider *p=2* in case of Network_maxRate andProcessor_clockRate and *p=3* relative to Nework_delay and Memory_freeSpace. As so we consider that Network_maxRate and Processor_clockRate are more significant than Response_delay and Memory_freeSpace in making the decision for service adaptation. Results depicted in Fig. 4. They show that the policy *VideoChat* is the most suitable adaptation strategy.

Several results have been also obtained using Minkowsky fitness function by considering different values of p and r. From those results, we realize that properly assigning values to these parameters will make Minkowsky distance-based fitness function much better to response to the current context. A systematic solution for automatically choosing the right values of elements of p and r is required; however it will lead to an optimization problem. Furthermore, selecting the best suitable fitness function could provide better adaptation policies to the actual context and user preferences.

Table 4. SRD(P'_1) and SRD(P'_2)

		$c_1, high$	$c_2, high$	$c_3, high$	c_4, low
SRD(P'_1)	SRD(p_1^1)	0,12	0,33	0,08	0,15
	SRD(p_1^2)	0,46	0,72	0,50	0,48
	SRD(p_1^3)	0,80	0,90	0,92	0,90
SRD(P'_2)	SRD(p_2^1)	0,06	0,10	---	0,15
	SRD(p_2^2)	0,20	0,23	---	0,23
	SRD(p_2^3)	0,20	0,57	---	0,58
	SRD(p_2^4)	0,54	0,47	---	0,40
	SRD(p_2^5)	0,54	0,90	---	0,83

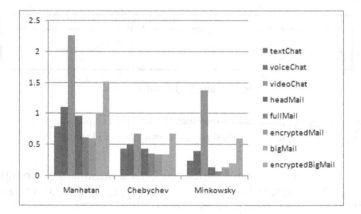

Fig. 4. Fitness degrees for service policies

5   Conclusions and Future Work

In this paper, we use QoS parameters and policies in both service selection and adaptation. The selection process allows getting the best-fitting services while the second is used for customizing the selected service to the actual context. The model represents QoS requirements and user preferences with fuzzy sets to allow mimicking the human manner in expressing desires and performing the aggregations. Ongoing work tackles the adaption issues in which parameters and the required fitness function could be automatically selected according to the context and user preferences.

References

1. Zhou, C., Chia, L.-T., Lee, B.S.: Semantics in Service Discovery and QoS Measurement. IT Professional 7(2), 29–34 (2005)
2. Chaari, S.: Youakim. B., Biennier, F.: Enhancing Web Service Selection by QoS-Based Ontology and WS-Policy. In: SAC 2008 Proceedings (2008)
3. Madkour, M., El Ghanami, D., Maach, A.: QoS-based approach for context-aware service selection with fuzzy preferences handling. JCAT 47(4), 379–391 (2013)
4. Madkour, M., El Ghanami, D., Maach, A.: Context-Aware Service Adaptation: An Approach Based on Fuzzy Sets and Service Composition. J. Inf. Sci. Eng. 29(1), 1–16 (2013)
5. Bakhouya, M., Campbell, R.H., Coronato, A., De Pietro, G., Ranganathan, A.: Introduction to special section on formal methods in pervasive computing. ACM Transactions on Autonomous and Adaptive Systems 7(1), 6 (2012)
6. Lee, K., Jeon, J., Lee, W., Jeong, S., Park, S.: QoS For Web Services: Requirements and Possible Approaches. Technical report, W3C, Note 25, Web Services Architecture Working Group (2003)
7. Yu, W.D., Radhakrishna, R.B., Pingali, S., Kolluri, V.: Modeling the measurements of QoS requirements in web service systems. Simulation Journal 83(1), 75–91 (2007)
8. Dumas, M., García-Bañuelos, L., Polyvyanyy, A., Yang, Y., Zhang, L.: Aggregate Quality of Service Computation for Composite Services. In: Maglio, P.P., Weske, M., Yang, J., Fantinato, M. (eds.) ICSOC 2010. LNCS, vol. 6470, pp. 213–227. Springer, Heidelberg (2010)
9. Bunke, H., Shearer, K.: A graph distance metric based on the maximal common subgraph. Pattern Recognition Letters 19, 255–259 (1998)
10. Grigori, D., Corrales, J.C., Bouzeghoub, M., Gater, A.: Ranking bpel processes for service discovery. IEEE Transactions on Services Computing 3, 178–192 (2010)
11. Yage, R.R.: Families of OWA operators. Fuzzy Sets and Systems 59, 125–148 (1993)
12. Yang, S.W., Shi, M.L.: A model for Web service discovery with QoS Constraints. Chinese Journal of Computers 28(4), 589–594 (2005)
13. Guo, D.K., Ren, Y., Chen, H.H.: A QoS-Guaranteed and Distributed Model for Web Service Discovery. Journal of Software 17(11), 2324–2334 (2006)
14. Ran, S.: A Model for Web Services Discovery with QoS. SIGecom Exchange 4, 1–10 (2003)
15. Lee, K.C., Jeon, J.H., Lee, W.S., Jeong, S.H., Park, S.W.: QoS for Web Services: Requirements and Possible Approaches. W3C Working Group Note 25 (2003)
16. Weiser, M.: Hot topics: Ubiquitous computing. IEEE Computer (1996)
17. Bakhouya, M., Gaber, J.: Approaches to Ubiquitous Computing. In: Labiod, H. (ed.) Wireless Ad hoc and Sensor Networks, pp. 111–142. ISTE Publishing Knowledge/John Wiley and Sons Inc., London (2008)
18. Cao, J., Xing, N.: Service adaptation using fuzzy theory in context-aware mobile computing middleware. In: Proceedings of the 11th IEEE Conference on Embedded and Real-Time Computing Systems and Applications, pp. 496–501 (2005)
19. Kruskal, J.B.: Multidimensional scaling by optimizing goodness of fit to a non metric hypothesis. Psychometrika 29(1), 1–27 (1964)
20. Stenström, P.: High performance embedded architectures and compilers. In: Third International Conference HiPEAC, Göteborg, Sweden (2008)
21. Abello, J.M., Pardalos, P.M., Mauricio, G.C.: Handbook of Massive Data Sets. Springer (2002) ISBN 1402004893
22. Dijkman, R., Dumas, M., Van Dongen, B., Käärik, R., Mendling, J.: Similarity of business process models: Metrics and evaluation. Inf. Syst., 498–516 (2011)

Privacy-Aware Business Processes Modeling Notation (PrvBPMN) in the Context of Distributed Mobile Applications

Wadha Labda, Nikolay Mehandjiev, and Pedro Sampaio

Centre for Services Research,
University of Manchester,
Manchester, UK
wadha.labda@postgrad.manchester.ac.uk,
{n.mehandjiev,P.Sampaio}@manchester.ac.uk

Abstract. Distributed mobile applications are increasingly being considered as solutions which provide robustness and performance benefits, especially in contexts such as emergency response systems, where a conventional centralized ICT infrastructure can be rendered inoperative. The information intensive nature of such systems brings to the fore the importance of data distribution through the right workflow channels under conditions of data privacy and short timescales. This paper reports on the early stages of a project aimed at developing a privacy-aware process-level framework for such distributed mobile applications, exemplified through a distributed prototype that can be used to model and manage fire emergency situations in airports. The novelty of the framework arises from modeling, reasoning and generating privacy preserving business processes applicable to distributed mobile information systems.

Keywords: privacy modelling, BPMN, privacy-aware, service-based.

1   Introduction

With the increasing number of natural and man-made disasters, modeling and development of emergency response systems is becoming a key priority for governments and corporations across the globe towards mitigating the impact of natural disasters and/or terrorist attacks. Due to the dynamic, information intensive and life critical nature of emergency response systems, access and management of resources such as data, software applications and human resources need to be securely, effectively coordinated and timely. To address this issue, many researchers have been considering distributed mobile applications as solutions for such emergency situations [11], due to its ability to provide robustness and performance benefits. Emergency situations in airports are considered one of the complex scenarios that need specially designed solutions to handle communications and coordination successfully between different actors participating in the management and rescue response. An excellent interpretation of emergency management was given by [24] which is "getting the

M. Matera and G. Rossi (Eds.): MobiWIS 2013 Workshops, CCIS 183, pp. 120–134, 2013.
© Springer International Publishing Switzerland 2013

right resources to the right place at the right time to provide the right information to the right people to make the right decisions at the right level at the right time". Successful planning and design of emergency management systems could achieve this. One of the key issues system designers must keep in mind while designing mobile distributed solutions for systems is privacy. Failing in correctly defining privacy requirements in a system could cause the failure of whole system. Privacy requirements and constraints must be modeled during design-time and enforced at runtime [16]. There is indeed a body of work on business processes privacy [2][6] yet they did not consider the requirements arising out of mobile context.

In this paper the emergency situation at airports is considered an example of target application domain. It needs specially designed solutions to handle communications and coordination successfully between different actors participating in the management and rescue response. They are expected to use mobile technologies to exchange the evacuation plans and requests for assistance. Key issues to be tackled in the solution design relate to risks related to information leakages and unauthorized use and access to private data in emergency situations [10]. To capture all the requirements of the emergency situation in a conceptual representation that is understood by all stakeholders, business process modeling [21] is used to model such emergency situation processes and define the communications and interaction of different activities. BPMN is used since it supports conceptual descriptions of emergency workflows and it can be used to generate executable code from process specifications. Moreover, it is easy to be understood and analyzed by managers and business stakeholders [6].

A privacy-aware framework and a method for constructing mobile distributed systems are needed to solve this problem. This research is investigating the different approaches that can be developed to address privacy in process-level notations in distributed service systems, and aiming to complement systems analysis and design approaches with tailored techniques for modeling and reasoning about privacy issues that can enable model checking of privacy constraints in distributed service systems.

This paper introduces a work in progress in this direction. A case study on airport fire emergency management system using passenger's mobile devices is presented. This paper is structured as following: Section 2 presents a background about the notions and technologies that is used to develop our approach. Section 3 presents a motivating example on Airport fire emergency situations and the challenges related to it, how to represent the situation using BPMN, then present the privacy requirements related to the target domain. Section 4 presents the initial details of our work in progress approach, and it shows an example of applying our approach to the fire emergency situation. Section 5 discusses related work and identifies the gap that our work is addressing. Section 6 describes the conclusions and future work.

2   Motivating Example

The following is a scenario that motivates our research and from which we will extract privacy requirements for emergency response in distributed mobile information systems.. The selected scenario is a critical fire emergency situation at Airports.

The following section will present the general business process of the airport scenario. Then the challenges and privacy requirements will be discussed. After that, a process-level representation of the scenario will be given. Moreover, some of the related work on process-level emergency management systems will be discussed.

2.1   Airport Fire Emergency Scenario: General Business Process

A fire occurs on the airport ground. The fire affects the emergency control unit, so no communication can be transferred from there. Luckily the airport has a backup plan of using smart phones as a media for communication. These handsets belong to the people in charge of emergency control, and could include the handsets of airport passengers, which will increase privacy concerns. A prompt and efficient solution must be reached which will save peoples' lives, airport resources and preserve privacy of all parties. In case of a fire emergency on Airport location, there are a standard procedure steps to manage such emergencies. These steps are emergency detection, emergency response and emergency response evaluation. Each step has its own sub-processes shown in Figure 1. To enable the use of passengers' mobile devices in an emergency situation, one scenario could be downloading specially designed application to the passengers' mobile devices' systems that will automatically sense the fire alarm and act based on it. This could be downloaded when user purchase and download their tickets. The system will ask them to if they would like to participate in evacuation plan if a fire emergency occurs at the airport.

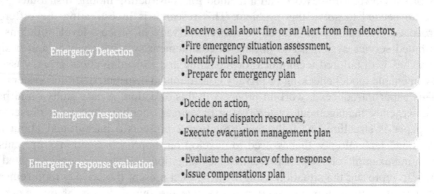

Fig. 1. Emergency Response Sub-Processes

2.2   Process-Level Representation of Airport Emergency Scenario

Key to the Success of an emergency response system is the quick and reliable response. For this purpose the use of BPMN modeling provides an effective approach that ensures emergency response processes are clearly defined and easy to be followed. BPMN defines the syntax of the process and specifies messages and information flows between participants in the process. Refer to [3] for more information on BPMN. A key limitation of BPMN for modeling emergency is its lack of ability to provide the semantics of the modeled system. However, it provides an intuitive notation that can be mapped to formal constructs to support model checking and reasoning. Figure 6 below is a partial representation of airport emergency response management situation pointing out possible privacy issues. Association of privacy constraints in modeling emergency situations ensures that the system will be aware of privacy constraints and enforce them when a realistic emergency situation occurs.

3   Background

This section will present a background on the technologies that will be used in our approach. First, the business processes and BPMN is discussed. Then, a definition of privacy and its dimensions is presented.

3.1   Business Processes

We implement and get engaged in business processes in our daily life either being us as the requester of services or the provider. A business process is a set of activities that may need more that one entity to work collaboratively to achieve a business objective [4]. Business process Management (BPM) [21] has been utilized as one of software engineering technologies that is used to model system requirements and processes. With the rapid growth of businesses and technologies, it has become a necessity for business managers', decision makers and software designers to closely collaborate and participate in the designing processes of a given system. BPM defines the syntax of the process and specifies messages and information flows between participants in the process. A key limitation of BPM for modeling business processes is its lack of ability to provide the semantics of the modeled system [21]. However, it provides an intuitive notation that can be mapped to formal constructs to support model checking and reasoning. Moreover, BPM are considered central information storage [15]. For this reason, all relevant information should be included or at least linked to the models. There are many existing modeling languages that differ in expressiveness and semantics such as Business Process Modeling Notation (BPMN) [3], Event Driven Process Chain (EPC)[22], Petri Nets [13], and UML Activity Diagrams (AD) [16]. In this research we will use BPMN as the formal modeling language for our research. The rationale behind this is that BPMN can be extended easily to support system semantics.

3.2   Business Process Modeling Notation (BPMN)

To achieve a successful integration and a system with competitive advantage, system designers and developers should find a modeling method that supports agility and change management. For this purpose the use of BPMN modeling provides an efficient approach that ensures processes are clearly defined and easy to be followed [21]. BPMN defines the syntax of the process and specifies messages and information flows between participants in the process. BPMN diagrams have four main elements:

Flow objects, connection objects, artifacts, and swimlanes. Flow objects, such as activities, events, and gateways, define the process behavior. Connection objects define the messages flows between the flow objects, and there are three different types of connection objects: sequence flow, association and message flow. Data objects are considered as artifacts, and swimlanes define the different participants in the process [3]. BPMN does not express the semantics of the modeled system. However, it can be extended to support system semantics. That's why we are working on developing an extension to BPMN to enable semantic definitions of the process, and look into mapping these constructs to an execution language such as business process execution language (BPEL).

3.3   Privacy in Business Processes

In this section we will define what is privacy, present the different dimensions of privacy, and discuss the attributes of the two dimensions that we will cover in our privacy-aware approach.

3.3.1   What Is Privacy?
Privacy as a noun in the dictionary means "The state or condition of being free from being observed or disturbed by other people". Which means the right to be left alone. But this is used to work in the past when less information was tackled online. Now with the enormous amount of information collected every day, the need to provide information online increases and the risk of personal information being exposed or breached also increases [4].

Privacy usually concerns personal or sensitive data, which can be used to identify a person and the misuse of it could cause harm to that person [14]. It is a fundamental human right (Pearson, 2009). Nowadays, there are significant efforts to protect privacy using law and regulations such as Organization for Economic Co-operation and Development (OECD), which defines eight principles, and Federal Trade Commission of United States (FTC), as well as technical solutions [7]. The following sections will discuss privacy in more details specifying the different dimensions and attributes of each dimension.

3.3.2   Privacy Dimensions
When addressing privacy we are considering mainly four dimensions of personal privacy [5], which are Privacy of the person, *i.e.* physical privacy, which mainly concerns a person's physical body and its constituents. The second dimensions are Privacy of personal behavior that is mainly concerned with the privacy of a person behavior, referred to it as media privacy. The third dimension is Privacy of personal communications, which is concerned with freedom of Individuals to communicate using various media without being continuously monitored. The fourth dimension is the privacy of personal data, which protect personal data from being exposed to other individuals and organizations, and an individual must be able to have control over their data even if possessed by other parties. Figure 2 shows these four dimensions. Among the four dimensions, this research is interested in the last two dimensions,

Privacy of personal communication and privacy of personal data because they are more concerned with information system privacy. To be able to develop a framework addressing these two dimensions, a set of attributes that will be defining the privacy-preserving rule is defined below.   These attributes also will help to develop the visual privacy-preserving constructs as extensions to BPMN.

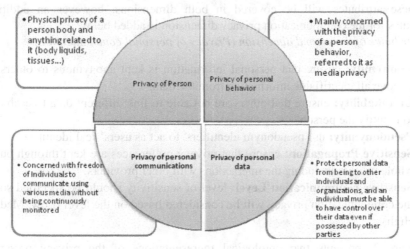

Fig. 2. Privacy Dimensions (Roger Clark, 1999)

Attributes of the first dimension (Privacy of personal data):.

o   **Data:** Describe Data categories used in communications or transition of systems or within a single system. They are usually defined in upper-level categories of data that is from privacy point of view will be treated differently. Such categories are:

*   Personal Identifier information: names, address, email addresses, device mac addresses
*   Sensitive information: Social security number, credit card number, medical data
*   Medium sensitivity information: personal information that is not considered as personal identifier such as gender, social relations.
*   Usage data: Browsing and transactions history
*   Public Data: Any data that is made public by users such as hobbies,

o   **Actor:** Describe the set of individuals or organizations who can access the data and they are distinct from a privacy point of view.

o   **Action:** Describes the activities performed on data (Collect, Read, Update, Disclose, Delete)

o   **Purpose:** Describe the purpose of collecting, using or disclosing data.

o   **Permissions:** Represent set of permissions granted to actors to access Data, Deontic-permissions (Permitted, Obligation, Forbidden, Permitted if condition true).

o   **Conditions:** Requirements that must be met for the actions to be allowed.

o   **Data Retention:** Defines the period of time the data is kept at the requested end. Such rules could be: delete once done with transaction, keep for personal analysis, indefinite.
o   **Enforcement mechanism:** Mechanisms that will be used to enforce privacy such as Policy (Laws and regulations), data encryption, Rules, …

These attributes will be covered in both dimensions, however an additional attributes for the communication privacy dimension is added below.
Attributes of the second dimension (Privacy of personal communication):.

o   **Anonymity:** ensure that personal information is kept anonymous to others, i.e. remove all identifiable information from the data.
o   **Unlinkability:** ensure that others are not able to link different data to each other to identify the person.
o   **Pseudonymity:** use pseudonym identifiers, to act as users' real identities
o   **Sensitive Propagation:** ensure that privacy preferences are kept through out the whole process including the interactions with other providers.
o   **Sensitive communication Level:** level of sensitivity should be specified so that the communication privacy will be considered based on the level (Low, Medium, High)

Figure 3, presents two ontological representations of the privacy preserving attributes for both dimensions.

3.4   Privacy Requirements of the Domain

The dynamic nature of emergencies makes the system vulnerable for intended and unintended privacy attacks from malicious users. Thus, identifying the privacy issues and constraints at the design phase, helps in reducing this vulnerability problem. In addition to this, we have to keep in mind, while addressing privacy issues, the functional requirements such as efficient and effective response especially in emergency response. Examples of these issues are: Personal information leakage from passengers' mobile devices, unauthorized access to airport systems confidential files and information, and Intruder or terrorist trying to access and link different personal data to identify users and miss use the data. Association of privacy constraints in modeling business processes ensures that the system will be aware of privacy constraints and enforce them.   The following are some privacy requirements of an emergency response management system:

*   **Access Control:** Access to resources as well as actions need to be restricted to certain roles or subjects. (PARBAC)
*   **Separation of Duty:** More than one subject is required to successfully complete the process.
*   **Binding of Duty:** The same subject needs to execute several tasks of a process.

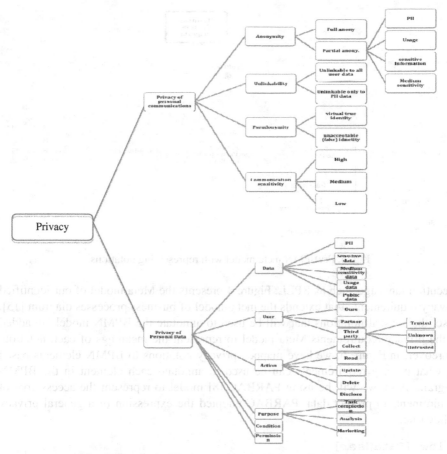

Fig. 3. Ontological Representations of Privacy Requirements

- **Necessity to Know:** A subject should only be able to access the information that is strictly necessary for completing a certain task.
- **Privacy preserving actions** such as anonymization or pseudonymization and Unlinkablity.
- **Purpose binding:** Data collected for one purpose should not used for another purpose without user consent)

4   Our Privacy-Aware Approach

Modeling privacy requirements on the process level requires the extension of the process modeling language (BPMN) with privacy concepts. Our approach is extending BPMN Meta model with formal constructs for the privacy requirements we specified before. We have developed ontology to represent each construct and used Semantic Web Rule Language (SWRL) [18] to represent the different rules and constraints on the BPMN notations. SWRL will help us to automate the transformation to

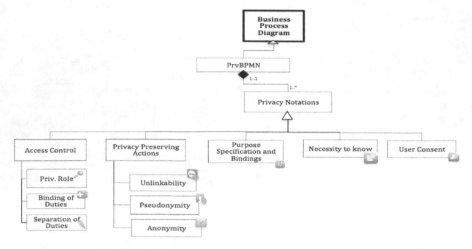

Fig. 4. PrvBPMN meta model with representing notations

execution language such as BPEL. Figure 4 presents the Meta model of our identified privacy requirements that extends the meta model of business processes diagram [15]. Also, their visual notations that will be used to annotate the BPMN model are added in the privacy requirements Meta model to represent the meanings of each notation. Moreover, in Figure 5, we have mapped privacy notations to BPMN elements based on what privacy requirements can be used to annotate each element in the BPMN diagram. Also, we will be using PARBAC [8] model to represent the access control requirements to protect data. PARBAC adopted the expression of a general privacy policy rule:

```
allow [DataUser]
to perf orm [Operation] on [DataT ype]
for [Purpose] provided [Condition]
carry out [Obligation]
```

Our access control rules are following the same format. Following is an example:

```
allow [user]
to perform [access] on [resources]
for [assistInER] provided [nessecaryAndnoIdentifiable]
carry out [notUseItForOtherPurposes]
```

The above rule is saying that "When in an airport emergency, a general user can access only necessary not identifiable resources to assist in emergency response (ER). Users should not be able to link available resources to other to be used for other purposes". Presenting the rule using PARBAC will make it easier for us to transform it to a formal reasoning language like SWRL, for compliance checking and privacy enforcement. The following is a SWRL representation of the above rule, where u is the user, x is the requested to access resource.

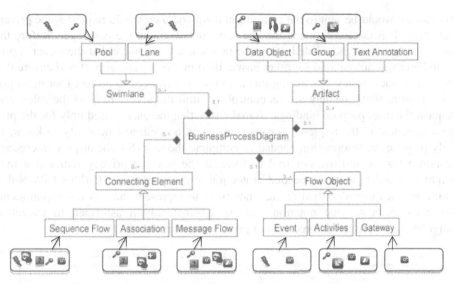

Fig. 5. Mapping of BPMN Elements to Privacy Notations

```
isEmergency(Airport)
^ resourceAccess(?x,?u)
^ locatedIn(?x, Airport)
^ hasStatus(?x, Anonymized)
-> hasOtherLinkedData(?x, ?u, Unlinkable)
```

Moreover, unexpected and exceptional situations tend to happen during emergency situations, which need some special ways of handling them to ensure that they would not cause any issues with privacy. So, to handle exceptional situations easily, it can be represented as events, in this case we will use Event Condition Action (ECA) [12] rules to allow treating them just like not exceptional situations. This part is still under investigation but we have chosen to develop it using ECA rules [12] since we find it a suitable language to address our research objectives. In the following section we will present an application of our approach to the scenario discussed in the previous sec-tion.

4.1   Application of Approach to Specify the Privacy Requirements in the Target Domain

In this section we will present an application of our approach to the Airport emergency situation. We used BPMN to visualize the fire response business process using BPMN. However, we did not present the full process due to space limitations. In Figure 6 we identified four main roles, namely, airport, fire department, medical services, and passengers of the airport. Each role will perform certain activities; some of these activities will have the potential to cause privacy leakages, specially the ones that need personal information such as name, age, location, etc. to complete their tasks. An example illustrated in Figure 6, is when a passenger requests for evacuation plans, his request would be sent to the evacuation team and they would request some private details such as the location and may be some details about the passenger. Before the passenger provides the needed details he or she needs to ensure that their data is protected and will not be used for other unspecified purposes. The airport will ensure that in their privacy policy. So, during this activity we will need to protect four main privacy requirements, namely access control, to limit the access only to the roles who request the data, purpose bindings, to make sure that the data is used only for the purpose specified in the request, user consent, when needed, and necessity to know, to only provide the information needed to complete the task. So, the airport emergency response team could use our tool to forecast the possible privacy issues that they might face and prepare the needed protection to every situation. On this BPMN diagram we used our identified privacy notations to represent the privacy requirements for each element. That notation will be automatically transformed to execution language to ensure the enforcement of privacy requirements.

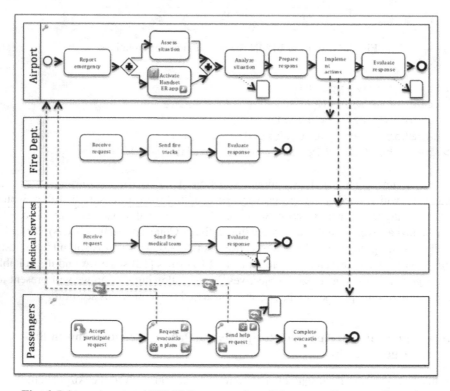

Fig. 6. Privacy Annotated BPMN Representation of Emergency Response Scenario

5   Related Work

The following two sections will discuss some related work on Privacy and BPMN and also existing work on modeling emergency systems.

5.1   BPMN and Privacy

Among the well-known efforts in this area is the work of [2], they developed a model-driven framework for web services life cycle management called Servicemosaic. It has three main components: (1) Model representation and manipulation, (2) Analysis and management component, and (3) Development environment. Servicemosaic allows system designers to model privacy aspects using web service protocol. Using extended state machine model, the use and storage of personal information descriptions are integrated with a web service protocol. Privacy aspects such as data collection, disclosure, access, and retention of web service protocols are modeled with this proposed conceptual model. However, there is no support for BPEL code generation; the authors claim that as a future work. Another equally important work is done by [6], which is a platform for process modeling on the web called ORYX. The main aim for this platform is to be extensible and to be used by BPM community. It will help researchers to find a tool ready to be extended to address their research questions. This platform is an influential modeling base for the researchers. However, the authors did not show any work on privacy or any non- functional requirements. Furthermore, [1] presented a work on specifying compliance rules visually and explaining their violations for business processes. They use a pattern-based approach to utilize a visual language (BPMN-Q). [4] have presented a work called SecureBPMN, where they extend visually the BPMN with privacy requirements (Access control, separation of duty, binding of duty and need to know) and enforce it during run time using XACML. SecureBPMN allows for specifying role-based access control (RBAC) as well as other security and compliance properties. RBAC is specified using separate interface while separation and binding of duty is added as components to BPMN visual diagram. In similar fashion with [2] and [4], this research will provide a modeling extension for privacy concerns such as authentication, access control and openness and transparency. Moreover, it will work on a novel technique to reason and transform privacy visual constructs to executable languages.

5.2   Related Work to Emergency Modeling

Managing emergencies requires a considerable amount of heterogeneity across different actors, resources and systems participating in the response and rescue, such as fire departments, medical services departments and so on [22]. Thus, designing a system that is web service-based is considered one of the best possible solutions. The capabilities of the service-oriented models support integration of heterogeneous application interfaces and the exchange of messages between systems on demand. One of the examples of some existing work using web services to implement emergency management systems are in [22], the proposed the EVResponse application which make use of web services to provide to both decision makers and first response unite a real-time reporting capabilities. They define a tier for web services to integrate different applications and enhance the emergency response techniques. In line with that, [15] emphasize the benefits of using web services to coordinate emergency response activities. Moreover, [17] proposed emergency management application, which is a decision support system that is based on the technology of semantic web services, which will help users to get the needed information more quickly and accurately. The above approaches are just examples of the huge amount of use of web services to facilitate the integration of different systems and help in getting the results more efficiently.

Recently, business process modeling is used to model such emergency situations processes and define the communications and interaction of different activities. The reason for using BPM is that it supports agility, easy to change when needed, and it would be on an application independent level. Moreover, it is easy to be understood and analyzed by managers and business stakeholders [7]. For example, [7] proposed a method to model a web service-based system using Petri net to logically describe the composite web services and they have highlighted the logical modeling usefulness in ensuring the correctness of the system. Most of the existing work used Petri Net to model emergency situations, because of its support to semantics and its underlying algebra, which makes it easier to formally verify the correctness of their models. However, when it comes to modeling non-functional or privacy constraints, it can be complex and confusing to use Petri net because it lacks support to model non-functional requirements [7]. In addition, none of the existing work considered privacy issues in emergency situations, most of the work were focusing on how to model, analyze and verify the modeling methods. The gap in the literature gives an important value to our work, were we will be working on modeling privacy constraints keeping in mind the nature of the emergency situation with unreliable network connections and heterogeneity of mobile devices with its special design requirements. A novel privacy preserving approach to service compositions will be developed, that will allow first to model the problem in BPMN and dynamically generate the underlying formal constructs that will work on reasoning and model checking the correctness and reliability of the model.

6   Conclusion and Future Work

The gap in the literature gives an important value to our work, modeling privacy constraints, keeping in mind the nature of the emergency situation with unreliable network connections and heterogeneity of mobile devices with its special design requirements. Our aim is to develop a privacy-aware service-based framework and system that will be used to model and manage fire emergency situations in airports and can be also extended to other situations. A novel privacy preserving extension to BPMN approach will be developed, that will allow first modeling the problem in BPMN and dynamically generating the underlying formal constructs that will work on reasoning and model checking the correctness and reliability of the model. For this research problem to be addressed it will need a structured approach to build and evaluate the framework to ensure it has rigor and relevance. Hence, the Design Science approach will be employed to address the research problem. The specific model of Design Science research to be used in this research is that presented by Hevner et al. (2004). The future research tasks of this project are shown in the following steps:

First, develop a complete BPMN representation tool of the Airport scenario including all privacy constraints. While addressing privacy issues, functional requirements such as efficient and effective response must be taken into account. This extension to BPMN must be verified and checked. Therefore, a privacy-aware model checker will be developed based on existing formal constructs. A prototype will also be developed to test and validate the framework.

References

1. Awad, A., Weidlich, M., Weske, M.: Visually specifying compliance rules and explaining their violations for business processes. Journal of Visual Languages & Computing 22(1), 30–55 (2011)
2. Benatallah, B., Reza, H., Nezhad, H.R.M., Casati, F., Toumani, F., Ponge, J.: Service Mosaic: A Model- Driven Framework for Web Services Life-Cycle Management. IEEE Internet Computing 10(4), 55–63 (2006)
3. Business Process Modeling notation (BPMN), version 1.2, Object Management Group (OMG) (January 2009)
4. Brucker, A.D., Hang, I.: Secure and Compliant Implementation of Business Process-Driven Systems. In: La Rosa, M., Soffer, P. (eds.) BPM 2012 Workshops. LNBIP, vol. 132, pp. 662–674. Springer, Heidelberg (2013)
5. Clarke, R.: Introduction to dataveillance and information privacy, and definitions of terms (1999), http://www.anu.edu.au/people/Roger.Clarke/DV/Intro.html
6. Decker, G., Overdick, H., Weske, M.: Oryx- Sharing Conceptual Models on the Web. In: Li, Q., Spaccapietra, S., Yu, E., Olivé, A. (eds.) ER 2008. LNCS, vol. 5231, pp. 536–537. Springer, Heidelberg (2008)
7. Han, R., Liu, K., Ju, Y., Zhao, J.: A Petri net theory-based method for modeling web service-based systems. In: 4th WiCOM, Dalian, China, pp. 1–7 (2008)
8. He, Q.: Privacy Enforcement with an Extended Role-Based Access Control Model, North Carolina State University at Raleigh, Raleigh, NC (2003)
9. Hevner, A., March, S., Park, J., Ram, S.: Design Science in Information Systems Research. MIS Quarterly 28(1), 75–106 (2004)
10. Landau, S.: Security and privacy landscape in emerging technologies. IEEE Security & Privacy 6(4), 74–77 (2008)
11. Landgren, J., Nulden, U.: A study of emergency response work: patterns of mobile phone interaction. In: Proceedings of the SIGCHI Conference on Human Factors in Computing Systems, pp. 1323–1332 (2007)
12. Poulovassilis, A., Papamarkos, G., Wood, P.T.: Event-condition-action rule languages for the semantic web. In: Grust, T., et al. (eds.) EDBT 2006 Workshops. LNCS, vol. 4254, pp. 855–864. Springer, Heidelberg (2006)
13. Peterson, J.L.: Petri net theory and the modeling of systems. Prentice-Hall (1981)
14. Pearson, S.: Taking Account of Privacy When Designing Cloud Computing Services. In: ICSE Workshop on Software Engineering Challenges of Cloud Computing, CLOUD 2009, pp. 44–52 (2009)
15. Rodríguez, A., Fernández-Medina, E., Piattini, M.: A BPMN Extension for the Modeling of Security Requirements in Business Processes. IEICE - Transactions on Information and Systems E90-D(4), 745–752 (2007)

16. Russell, N., van der Aalst, W.M.P., ter Hofstede, A.H.M., Wohed, P.: On the Suitability of UML 2.0 Activity Diagrams for Business Process Modelling. In: Third Asia-Pacific Conference on Conceptual Modelling (APCCM 2006). CRPIT, vol. 53, pp. 95–104 (2006)

17. Song, Y.J., Lee, D.H., Yim, J.G., Nam, T.Y.: Privacy Aware Adaptable Web Services Using Petri Nets. In: Proceedings of the 2007 International Conference on Convergence Information Technology (ICCIT 2007), pp. 1933–1938. IEEE Computer Society, Washington, DC (2007)

18. Semantic Web Rule Language (SWRL) (May 2004),
    http://www.w3.org/Submission/SWRL/

19. Tanasescu, V., Gugliotta, A., Domingue, J., Davies, R., Gutiérrez-Villarías, L., Rowlatt, M., Richardson, M., Stinčić, S.: A semantic web services GIS based emergency management application. In: Cruz, I., Decker, S., Allemang, D., Preist, C., Schwabe, D., Mika, P., Uschold, M., Aroyo, L.M. (eds.) ISWC 2006. LNCS, vol. 4273, pp. 959–966. Springer, Heidelberg (2006)

20. Thomas, M., Andoh-Baidoo, F., George, S.: Evresponse - moving beyond traditional emergency response notification. In: Proceedings of the Eleventh Americas Conference on Information Systems (2005)

21. van der Aalst, W.M.P., ter Hofstede, A.H.M., Weske, M.: Business Process Management: A Survey. In: van der Aalst, W.M.P., Weske, M. (eds.) BPM 2003. LNCS, vol. 2678, pp. 1–12. Springer, Heidelberg (2003)

22. Van der Aalst, W.M.P.: Formalization and verification of event-driven process chains Inform. Software Technol. 41(10), 639–650 (1999)

23. Xiaofeng, Y., Sommestad, T., Fung, C., Hung, P.C.K.: Emergency Response Framework for Aviation XML Services on MANET. In: Web Services, ICWS 2008, pp. 304-311 (2008)

24. Xu, W., Zlatanova, S.: Ontologies for Disaster Management Response. In: Li, J., Zlatanova, S., Fabbri, A. (eds.) Geomatics Solutions for Disaster Management, pp. 185–200 (2010)

On the Use of Location-Based Services and Geofencing Concepts for Safety and Road Transport Efficiency

Ahmed Nait-Sidi-Moh[1], Wafaa Ait-Cheik-Bihi[2],
Mohamed Bakhouya[3], Jaafar Gaber[4], and Maxime Wack[4]

[1] Université de Picardie Jules Verne, 48 Rue Raspail, 02100, Saint-Quentin, France
ahmed.nait-sidi-moh@u-picardie.fr
[2] Itris Automation Square, Square Roger Genin Grenoble, France
wait@automationsquare.com
[3] Aalto University, FIN-00076 Aalto, Finland
mohamed.bakhouya@aalto.fi
[4] Universite de Technologie de Belfort-Montbéliard, 90010 Belfort Cedex, France
{gaber,maxime.wack}@utbm.fr

Abstract. Advanced systems to assist drivers and increase road safety and efficiency are developed in recent years using new technologies, such as navigation systems, embedded systems, communication technologies, and web-based applications. However, the implementation of new solutions using these technologies requires concepts based on information and resources sharing and inter-services communication. Sharing information between services allows acquiring more knowledge about the current events on the road that helps participants making appropriate decisions. The paper introduces a service-oriented platform integrating Geofencing techniques for real-time tracking of mobile devises. A prototype was developed and deployed within the EU project ASSET-Road[1], and preliminary experiment results are reported to show the feasibility and the impact of this solution on safety and road transport efficiency.

Keywords: Geofencing, Web services, Location-based services, Service composition, Navigation systems, Communication technologies.

1 Introduction

Advanced cooperative systems using new technologies are needed to assist drivers and increase road transport safety and efficiency. Communication technologies combined with global navigation satellite systems (GNSS) are among the powerful technologies that can be used to meet the new safety challenge and transport efficiency. However, the design and implementation of collaborative systems using distributed architectures aiming to compose various services that interact and cooperate to accomplish certain tasks is required. For example, among techniques and approaches used are service-oriented architecture (SOA) principles [1, 2].

---

[1] http://www.project-asset.com

M. Matera and G. Rossi (Eds.): MobiWIS 2013 Workshops, CCIS 183, pp. 135–144, 2013.
© Springer International Publishing Switzerland 2013

In this work, an interoperable and cooperative platform [10], based on Web-service principles and Geofencing techniques [11], is used for real-time tracking of mobile devices. The platform uses mobile and embedded communication systems, positioning and navigation techniques using GNSS, and techniques and standards of web services [12]. The objective is to share information and ensure the synchronization and the coordination between involved services.

In this work, we focus mainly on the development and the integration of a geofencing application and its related services into a unified platform in order to allow defining virtual perimeters and controlling mobile devices. The remainder of this paper is organized as follows. Section 2 presents the related works. Geofencing prototype and preliminary results from real experiments are reported in Section3. Finally, Section 4 gives some conclusions and future work.

2   Related Work

New communication technologies and navigation satellite systems for business services collaboration and composition have recently attracted extensive research and development [5, 7]. GNSS systems and location-based services are used for information and navigation services to provide end-users with required information. These technologies are also used in emergency assistance where the location of mobile users in case of distress is provided. For example, approximately 5000 lives could be saved each year in the Europe with automatic positioning of emergency calls using E-112 [8][2] with the intention of the European Commission to mandate the emergency call by the end of 2015, and E-911 in USA [9]. Another application of these technologies concerns tracking and monitoring services. For these business services, the system consists of GNSS receiver integrated with GSM/GPRS module and embedded into the vehicle for V2I communications [3, 6, 7]. Other tracking applications have been recently developed, such as taxi monitoring and dispatching, workforce management, mobile supply-chain management, child support and security, tracking of elderly persons, and goods and package tracking [5].

However, business services are developed independently from each other and there are no platforms or standardized architectures developed for making inter-service collaboration simple and automatic in order to better achieve specific goals and tasks. The development and the deployment of such approaches to combine distributed applications in heterogeneous environments and to compose various services can considerably provide to users added-value services and relevant information [4, 10]. Furthermore, the use of information systems and communication technologies associated with GNSS and embedded systems represent a primordial task for development of innovative solutions for mobility management and road transport. GNSS systems provide vehicle positioning information and status of infrastructures, which can be accessed by service providers and end-users. The purpose of inter-service communication is to ensure the dissemination of the pertinent information for all local services in order to improve road safety, such as car accident avoidance [3, 7, 8]. In [6], two applications of automatic vehicle location applications have been developed. The first

---

[2] http://www.telefot.eu/

one concerns the management and control of fleet vehicles displacement for a public transportation company. In this application, a software package, integrating GNSS coupled with web Geographic Information System, was developed to manage and improve the efficiency of many operations in public transportation system, such as the optimization of services and transport costs, and the management of traffic and time schedules. The second application consists of a police traffic information system, wherein all information about an occurred accident should be localized and sent to the police station server via wireless communication. However, most applications developed in this context do not focus on collaboration and interaction between different location-based services and applications to provide more pertinent information.

In order to address this gap, a prototype platform, called TransportML, was developed and presented in [10], to enable collaboration between road-related services. Web service technology is used to develop actual LBSs in a standard and interoperable manner. TransportML platform interacts with mobile users using any technology allowing an Internet connection. In order to exchange data between services and the platform, a specific language, called *Transportation Markup Language* (TML), was developed to support these exchanges.

The work presented in this paper concerns the integration of Geofencing techniques for real-time tracking of mobile devices. Geofencing is an acronym of two words:*"fence"*, which means an enclosure or perimeter, and the prefix *"Geo"* which means that this perimeter is built from geographical data. *Geofence*can be then defined as the delimitation of a geographical area using a virtual perimeter. The idea of Geofencing or Geocorridor, is used in several applications based on GNSS systems [5]. It can be used, as depicted in Figure 1, to define a virtual perimeter around a geographic zone, and then to associate objects, such as vehicles or people, with this zone, and finally to generate an alarm when these objects cross the border of the perimeter.

Fig. 1. Detecting the entry of a mobile into a forbidden area

3   Geofencing Prototype and Experiments

3.1   Geofencing Prototype Architecture

Geofencing application operates and interacts with different location-based services using GNSS and communication technologies. The concept is based on an in-vehicle embedded device, which allows determining, and sending regularly its location to the management center. More precisely, each vehicle is equipped with an embedded computer, a GPS receiver, and a 3G communication module for data transmission. The in-vehicle embedded application receives data from the GPS receiver and sends it through the communication module to the server for processing. As illustrated in Figure 2, the Geofencing application runs on a server. Once the vehicle characteristics are registered in a database, its current position is known (using GPS/3G module embedded into the vehicle) and sent to server via internet relying on a network based on 3G. The management center is regularly informed about current positions of the registered vehicles. When, for example, a vehicle deviates from its allowed itinerary, the management center takes decisions and suggests appropriates solutions.

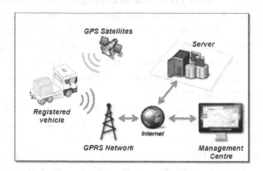

Fig. 2. The architecture of Geofencing application

3.2   Vehicle Compliance Verification

As previously mentioned, the adequate itinerary is computed and sent to the vehicle. The vehicle follows the suggested itinerary with a permanent display on a geographical map. The main issue is to verify if the vehicle follows the assigned itinerary. The vehicle compliance verification is illustrated in Figure 3. When a vehicle deviates from its geo-corridor, alerts are sent to the in-vehicle computer to warn the driver and to the management center to generate a new alternative itinerary.

The proposed algorithm allows supervising the vehicle motions. After registering the vehicle with its characteristics (e.g., departure point, destination, nature of transported goods), an adequate itinerary is defined by the platform while considering incoming information from all involved LBSs. This itinerary is saved as a sequence of points $(A_0, ..., A_N)$, with A_0 and A_N represent respectively the departure point and the vehicle's destination. As given in Figure 4, each two successive points A_i and A_{i+1} represent a section (line segment) of the itinerary.   A rectangle (Geofence) is formed from these two points whose the length and width are given, respectively, by S and $\overline{A_iA_{i+1}}$ (algebraic measure of the line segment $[A_iA_{i+1}]$). The non negative integer S represents a fixed threshold. A vehicle is represented by the point $M(X_M(t), Y_M(t))$ whose components are the Cartesian coordinates $(X_M(t), Y_M(t))$, which are calculated from GPS coordinates of the vehicle at time t. The translation method is detailed hereafter in Section 3.3. The vehicle's position $M(X_M(t), Y_M(t))$ is updated each Δt time units. We assume that during Δt (a short time) an eventual deviation of the vehicle from its itinerary will not be too large.

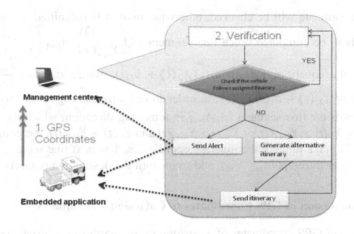

Fig. 3. Vehicle compliance verification

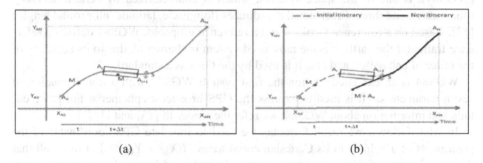

(a)   (b)

Fig. 4. The vehicle follows its assigned itinerary

Using the verification algorithm, the application checks if the vehicle position $M(X_M(t), Y_M(t))$ is inside or outside the defined rectangle from the two points $A_i(X_{Ai}(t), Y_{Ai}(t))$ and $A_{i+1}(X_{Ai+1}(t), Y_{Ai+1}(t))$ and the parameter S. By applying the algorithm, two cases are envisaged. If $M(X_M(t), Y_M(t))$ is inside the rectangle, this means that the vehicle follows the predefined itinerary by the application (Figure 4-a). Otherwise, the vehicle deviates from its Geo-corridor as illustrated in Figure 4-b. In this case, an alert is issued. The platform receives the current position of the vehicle, and invokes all services in order to compute a new itinerary from the received location. The current position M of the vehicle, which lies outside the rectangle, becomes A_0 and the algorithm restarts while considering the coordinates of the new position.

More precisely, monitoring the vehicle movement and checking if the vehicle moves inside or outside its predefined itinerary are based on the following process. It receives as inputs the coordinates $(A_0(X_{A0}(t), Y_{A0}(t))..., A_N(X_{AN}(t), Y_{AN}(t)))$, S, $X_M(t)$, $Y_M(t)$ and for each coordinate, it checks if $(X_{A_i}(t) \leq X_M(t) \leq X_{A_{i+1}}(t))$ OR $(Y_{A_i}(t) \leq Y_M(t) \leq Y_{A_{i+1}}(t))$ is valid, in this case if $Y_M(t) - \frac{Y_{A_{i+1}}(t) - Y_{A_i}(t)}{X_{A_{i+1}}(t) - X_{A_i}(t)} X_M(t) - b_i(t)) \leq S$

the next coordinate will be checked, otherwise an alert is submitted and a new itinerary needs to be computed. Each line segment $[A_i\begin{pmatrix}X_{A_i}(t)\\Y_{A_i}(t)\end{pmatrix}, A_{i+1}\begin{pmatrix}X_{A_{i+1}}(t)\\Y_{A_{i+1}}(t)\end{pmatrix}]$ is defined by the equation: $Y_A(t) = a_i(t) X_A(t) + b_i(t)$, where $a_i(t) = \frac{Y_{A_{i+1}}(t)-Y_{A_i}(t)}{X_{A_{i+1}}(t)-X_{A_i}(t)}$ and $b_i(t) = Y_{A_i}(t) - a_i(t)X_{A_i}(t)$. In order to optimize the algorithm, when the vehicle exceeds the line segment $[A_i\,A_{i+1}]$ in a moving direction, which means $X_M(t) > X_{Ai+1}(t)$, or $Y_M(t) > Y_{Ai+1}(t)$, or $X_M(t) > X_{Ai+1}(t)$ and $Y_M(t) > Y_{Ai+1}(t)$, the point A_i will be removed from the table of the itinerary coordinates. The next line segment to be considered and analyzed is $[A_{i+1,}A_{i+2}]$, and so on until the destination point A_N.

3.3   Conversion of GPS Coordinates to Cartesian Coordinates

Conversion of GPS coordinates of a position on the earth to Cartesian coordinates is based on Geodesic systems, also known as *datum*. World Geodesic System 1984 (WGS84), is one of the space systems, which is characterized by certain accuracy (one meter), and three-dimensional coordinates (longitude, latitude, ellipsoidal height) [13]. Based on a reference Geoid, using a reference ellipsoid, WGS84 defines a reference frame for the earth. It is the most used system in the world, due to its accuracy of the order of one meter, and also it is used by the GPS as a standard.

WGS84 is an extended version the first system WGS72 with a transformation of seven parameters. It is used to express the GPS broadcast ephemeris. For more details and information about WGS84, we refer the reader to [13] and [14].

In what follows, we recall formulas we used to translate GPS coordinates of the position M of a vehicle to its Cartesian coordinates $M(X_M(t), Y_M(t))$. Let us recall that decimal degrees of GPS coordinates express latitude and longitude geographic coordinates as decimal fractions and are used in many geographic information systems. GPS coordinates may be expressed in three ways:

- decimal degree : # *ddd.ddddd°*
- degrees and minutes decimals: # *ddd°mm.mmm'*
- degrees, minutes and seconds: # *ddd°mm'ss.sss"*

In order to obtain the Cartesian coordinates *(X,Y)* of a given position, we need first to convert its GPS coordinates *(# ddd°mm'ss.sss"* or one of other formats) into geographic coordinates *(λ, φ, h)* and then convert these last to Cartesian coordinates. If a vehicle position is expressed by GPS coordinates # *ddd°mm'ss.sss"*, these coordinates can be translated into the longitude *(λ)* and the latitude *(φ)* geographic coordinates according to the following expressions:

$$\text{Longitude} = \lambda = ddd°mm'ss.sss'' = ddd + \frac{mm}{60} + \frac{ss.sss}{3600} \tag{1}$$

$$\text{Latitude} = \varphi = ddd°mm'ss.sss'' = ddd + \frac{mm}{60} + \frac{ss.sss}{3600} \tag{2}$$

The third component *h* of geographic coordinates is the ellipsoidal height. This parameter is defined in a geodetic reference and may differ from the height of several tens of meters. According to the expressions of equations (1) and (2) and the parameter *h*, the Cartesian coordinates *(X, Y)* are given as follows:

$$X = (N + h) \, cos(\lambda) \, cos(\varphi) \tag{3}$$

$$Y = (N + h) \, sin(\lambda) \, cos(\varphi) \tag{4}$$

where : $N = \frac{a}{W}$, $W = \sqrt{1 - e^2 sin^2(\varphi)}$, $e^2 = \frac{a^2 - b^2}{a^2}$, *a* and *b* are constants and given according to the used geodesic system. For WGS84, the exact values of the two constants *a* and *b* are given by: *a = 6378137,0 m and b = 6356752,314245179 m* [13,14].

3.4   Experiment Results

Experiments are conducted based on a scenario with four web services that are developed, implemented and invoked via the platform. These services are defined as follows: *1) Road status* service which provides in real-time required information regarding the road status, *2) event recording service* which records events when the route status changes (e.g., accident, traffic jam). Using information provided by this service, Geofencing application informs vehicles and regenerates new itineraries, *3) Geofence service* which defines allowed and prohibited areas based on the registered vehicle characteristics, and *4) Itinerary computation service* which computes the fastest and safest itinerary. This service allows defining waypoints and advised and discouraged itineraries using information provided by all invoked services.

In order to compute an itinerary, the four defined Web services are involved and should interact with each other to give the most appropriate route depending on the vehicle characteristics. The various exchanges between these services, the platform, and the requester are illustrated in Figure 5. As illustrated in this figure, the proposed scenario is described as follows. To define a Geofence, the requester, *registered vehicle,* has to report all required information, such as the weight, the height, the transported goods, the limit speed, the type of vehicles needs to avoid while moving if the transported good is dangerous, etc. After verifying all these characteristics, Geofencing application communicates this information to the platform. The platform sends then the TML document to the *itinerary service* to calculate the adequate itinerary taking into account the content of TML document. Finally, the platform sends the defined Geo-corridor to the requester, and then proceeds to a tracking process of the vehicle travel from its origin to its destination.

A Web application for visualizing Geofences and defined itineraries on the map was developed. This application can be seen as a Web service client with a Web interface for map visualization. Figure 6 illustrates the use of Geofence service to define forbidden areas to be avoided using parameters, such as Geofence title, Geofence color, speed limit, maximum weight, and maximum height. Taking into consideration all these information, each area is defined by a colored polygon as displayed on the map and saved in a database in order to be considered when computing the required itinerary.

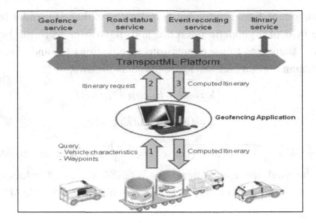

Fig. 5. Geofencing architecture

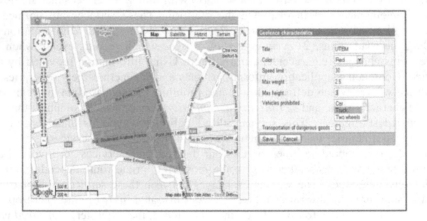

Fig. 6. Definition of Geofences

It is worth nothing that other types of Geofences can be used according the handled situation. For example, the surveillance of a geographical zone, which is accompanied by scheduled time slots. This means that the behavior of the geofence evolves in time. The Geofence may be active during certain time slots (at night for example) and inactive during the rest of the day. More details about other types of Geofences are presented in [11]. Figure 7(a) presents an example of computed itinerary without considering any forbidden or discouraged area. However, in order to avoid forbidden areas provided by invoked web services (road status for example), defined itinerary may be changed. With the aim to illustrate the feasibility and the consequence of the application, discouraged areas cover a part of the advised itinerary. As result, as shown in Figure 7(b), a new optimal itinerary is computed while avoiding forbidden areas.

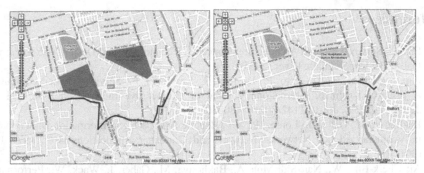

Fig. 7. Itinerary computation: (a) Without considering defined Geofences, (b) With Geofences

We have also developed an application for real-time tracking of snow plows using the geofencing concepts. The real-time positions of vehicles are shown in Figure 8. From experiments, we noticed that sometimes vehicle positions are inaccurate and exceed assigned itineraries. To correct GPS coordinates, the compliance verification algorithm is used to attach the current position of each vehicle to its trajectory based on the traveled distance and travel direction. The red lines represent the unclear sections and as long as the vehicles start removing snow, cleared sections become green.

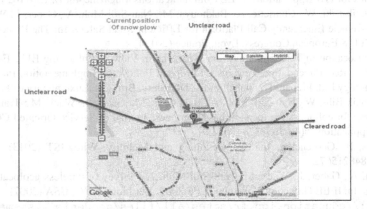

Fig. 8. Tracking of snow plows

4   Conclusions and Future Work

In this paper, a prototype of Geofencing application is developed and integrated into the TransportML platform for sharing road-related information. The application allows defining adequate and safe itineraries for specific vehicles. Each itinerary is computed and controlled while considering all provided information by other interacting services. A compliance verification algorithm is developed and tested. Some preliminary results are reported and show the feasibility and the effectiveness of using LBS interaction and Geofencing techniques. In the case of TDG, this solution might have a great impact on safety and road transport efficiency. Future work includes more experiments and the development of further services to be integrated into the platform.

References

1. Erl, T.: Service-Oriented Architecture: Concepts, Technology, and Design, 656 p. Prentice Hall PTR, Upper Saddle River (2005)
2. Papazoglou, M.-P., Traverso, P., Dustdar, S., Leymann, F.: Service-oriented computing: A research roadmap. International Journal of Cooperative Information Systems 17(2), 223–255 (2008), doi:10.1142/S0218843008001816.
3. Bakhouya, M., Gaber, J., Lorenz, P.: An Adaptive Approach for Information Dissemination in Vehicular Ad hoc Networks. Network and Computer Applications 34(6), 1971–1978 (2011)
4. Ait-Cheik-Bihi, W., Nait-Sidi-Moh, A., Bakhouya, M., Gaber, J., Wack, W.: Performance Study of Web Service Composition based on Formal Modeling of Workflow Patterns. In: 8th International Conference on Mobile Web Information Systems, Procedia Computer Science, vol. 10, pp. 728–735 (2012)
5. Nait-Sidi-Moh, A., Bakhouya, M., Gaber, J., Wack, M. (eds.): Geopositioning and Mobility. Wiley-ISTE (2013)
6. Sadoun, B., Al-Bayari, O.: Location based services using geographical information systems. J. Computer Communications 30(16), 3154–3160 (2007), doi:10.1016/j.comcom.2007.05.059
7. Dar, K., Bakhouya, M., Gaber, J., Wack, M., Lorenz, P.: Wireless Communication Technologies for ITS Applications. IEEE Communications Magazine 48(5), 156–162 (2010)
8. Ait-Cheik-Bihi, W., Chariette, A., Bakhouya, M., Nait-Sidi-Moh, A., Gaber, J., Wack, M.: An In-vehicle Emergency Call Platform for Efficient Road Safety. In: The Proceedings of the 8th ITS European Congress, Lyon, France (2011)
9. Caller Location in Telecommunication Networks in View of Enhancing E112 Emergency Services: Recommendation Towards a European Policy and Implementation Plan, Helios Technology Ltd. Prepared on behalf of the DGISiety, Brussels, Luxembourg (2002)
10. Ait-Cheik-Bihi, W., Nait-Sidi-Moh, A., Bakhouya, M., Gaber, J., Wack, M.: TransportML platform for collaborative location-based services. Journal of Service Oriented Computing and Applications 6(4), 363–378 (2012)
11. Reclus, F.: Geofencing. In: Geopositioning and Mobility. Wiley-IST (2013) ISBN-13: 978-1848215672
12. Roxin, A., Gaber, J., Wack, M., Nait-Sidi-Moh, A.: Survey of wireless geolocation techniques. In: IEEE Globcom/Workshop ICPS 2007, Washington DC, USA (2007)
13. http://education.ign.fr/sites/all/files/geodesie_systemes.pdf (last visit on July 2013)
14. Transformation entre systèmes géodésiques en France Métropolitaine. IGN/SGN/PMC report, V2.0 Copyright I.G.N. 1999/2009 (2009)

Author Index